The

Enchantingly Easy
Persian Cookbook

The Enchantingly Easy

Persian Cookbook

SIMPLE RECIPES FOR
BELOVED PERSIAN FOOD FAVORITES

Shadi HasanzadeNemati
Photography by Shannon Douglas

ROCKRIDGE
PRESS

A Paradise of Persian Favorites

Have you ever eaten at a Persian restaurant? The cuisine is rich and fragrant and exciting, and I'm guessing you loved it, or you wouldn't be looking at this book. But maybe you're thinking, "Oh, Persian food is really delicious, but it's too difficult to make."

Not really! That's why I wrote this book. In it, I will guide you through the journey of learning to make Persian food in very easy steps.

IF YOU ARE LOOKING FOR A WARM, THICK SOUP for cold evenings, check out Noodles & Herbs Ash (Ash-e-Reshteh) on page 78. It's filled with lentils and beans, and it's perfect for a cozy evening.

FEEL ADVENTUROUS? Try Pomegranate & Walnut Stew (Khoresh-e-Fesenjan) on page 87. The combination of tart pomegranate and buttery walnuts makes this stew extra delicious and tangy.

CRAVING KABOB but don't want to mess with the grill? Beef Pan Kabobs (Kabob Tabeh-i) on page 118 to the rescue. This dish uses ground beef and a special kneading method that's easy and effective. You'll have juicy Kabobs in no time.

DO YOU WANT TO KNOW ABOUT MY FAVORITE FOOD? It's Green Beans & Beef Mixed Rice (Loobia Polo) on page 165. I can have it every day and be happy! The combination of turmeric and cinnamon makes this dish magical.

IF IT'S WARM WHERE YOU ARE, make sure you're mixing up some Mint & Vinegar Syrup & Drink (Sharbat Sekanjabin) on page 186, with ice and cold water to avoid heat stroke and headaches.

MESMERIZE EVERYONE AROUND YOU by making the easy yet unbelievably delicious Saffron Syrup Cake (Keyk Sharbat Zaferan) on page 212. This cake is soaked in saffron syrup and smells like happiness!

CONTENTS

INTRODUCTION

I was born and raised in Tehran, the capital city of Iran. Tehran has become a melting pot of cultures and traditions as people from every part of the country have moved there, starting new stories of their own. You can hear someone speaking on the phone in Azeri (the old language of Azerbaijan) or two friends on the bus talking with Isfahani accents. (Isfahan, in central Iran, was once one of the largest cities in the world.) Blended families are common—the mother from Gilan on the Caspian Sea and the father from Zahedan in the southwest, near the Pakistani border, living in Tehran and visiting family on holidays. Each of these places has its own culture and traditions; even wedding rituals can differ from region to region.

My *maman* ("mother" in Farsi) was born in Tehran and my *baba* ("father" in Farsi) moved to Tehran at a very young age from Tabriz, a city in northwest Iran where people speak Azeri, a language similar to Turkish. My parents met in Tehran and started their family with two different cultures. It was an adventure to blend both. I grew up speaking Farsi and Azeri at home and learning English at school. Later I moved to Turkey, married my soulmate, and moved to his homeland, the United States. And all that moving around made me realize that wherever I am, Persian food has a special place in my heart—especially if it's made by my maman.

For many Iranians, their maman's food is the best Persian food, because it's made with so much love. I grew up in the kitchen. Every morning my maman would get up early, take a piece of chicken, beef, or lamb out of the freezer and defrost it in a bowl of cold water (microwaves were not very common), then start sautéing some finely chopped onions, because that's how many Persian recipes start. I always used to go into the kitchen and watch my maman's artistic hands moving so quickly and magically, creating a new miracle for that day. I would try to memorize every step and every spice, thinking how simple it is to make a tasty meal for the family in one pot with just a few ingredients.

Then the wonderful time of eating would come, when our family would sit on the floor around the table and enjoy delicious food made with fresh ingredients, patience, and love. We would talk about our day, what we were planning to do, and what made us happy—whether it was my parents planning our next holiday or my brother buying the newest video game. We would start with some salad or a bowl of plain yogurt topped with some dried mint. Then came rice, which was perfectly steamed, adorned with saffron, and accompanied by *Khoresh*, a type of stew.

Every Persian maman has her own recipes, passed on to her through generations. Not every family has the same recipe traditions; in my family, some of the traditional dishes are mixed chicken and barberry rice and mixed tuna and potato rice. One of my most favorite recipes, passed from my grandmother to my maman and then to me, is pan-seared fish made with a unique combination of spices. And following my family's tradition of respecting and blending the cultures in a marriage, I introduced Persian food to my husband, too, not just by cooking for him, but also by explaining why each spice is used and how each step is taken. Now he is a big fan of homemade Persian food, such as Barberry & Saffron Rice (page 110).

As you go through this cookbook, I hope you'll see that most Persian recipes have the same approach, and all end up being very delicious. The spices you need for Persian cooking are easy to find at local supermarkets, Middle Eastern and Arab stores, or even online, and as long as you have some freshly ground saffron, you are good to go. Persian food is also very healthy, and it can be easily adjusted to cater to special diets—or just to your taste.

Persian cuisine might seem intimidating, but I'm here to tell you that it's much easier than it looks to make Green Beans & Beef Mixed Rice (Loobia Polo) on page 165, Savory Saffron Rice Cake (Tahchin) on page 149, or even Chicken Kabobs (Joojeh Kabob) on page 116. A love of good food is all you need!

1 PERSIAN CUISINE MADE SIMPLE

To many, Persian food means lots of kabobs, lamb, saffron, and rice. But there is much more to this classic Middle Eastern cuisine that makes it unique. Persian cuisine has mild flavors. It includes all the food groups in every meal—proteins, grains, vegetables, and healthy fats. It's always made with fresh, seasonal ingredients, and it naturally lends itself to dietary restrictions such as meat-free, nut-free, and gluten-free.

Food has always been an important part of Persian culture. Recipes are treated like family heirlooms, and preparing and eating meals brings people together, builds teamwork, and honors simplicity and freshness while emphasizing beauty and technique. Like Persian carpets and art, Persian food is a culmination of natural ingredients, patience, and love.

FROM ANCIENT PERSIA TO MODERN IRAN

Persian cuisine has come a long way from *Khoresh Dehghani* (an ancient dish of salted lamb and mint marinated in pomegranate molasses and served with boiled eggs) to *salad olivieh* (a salad that came to Iran by way of Russia). Because Iran was located on the Silk Road trade route, which connected the East and the West from China to the Mediterranean Sea, its native Persian cuisine benefited from the many different cultures that passed through along the way. For instance, both Persian and Indian cuisines use turmeric, and the word *kofta* or *koofteh* refers to meatballs of different shapes and forms in both Iran and Turkey.

Food has always been a very important part of Persian daily life. Feasts and gatherings, whether simple ones with close family members and friends or big ones for shahs and sultans, have a long tradition. In ancient days, Persian women spent the majority of their days on household chores. Most Persian foods required a lot of preparation and many hours of cooking over low heat. The women would do the prep in the morning, and as the food was slowly simmering, they would do the rest of the housework, have some tea with their neighbors, and take care of their children.

Rice has been a staple of Persian cooking since the Safavid Dynasty in the sixteenth century. At that time, it was mainly grown and eaten by the wealthier families in the north. For everyone else, bread was the main staple. As time went on, rice became more widely cultivated and eventually emerged as the most important grain used in Persian cooking. It was usually served with some kind of stew made from chicken, beef, or lamb, plus vegetables and herbs, all cooked in a thick sauce for hours.

When a family invited guests to their home for a meal, the preparation would start a few days before, and sometimes the neighbors would come to help too. When the guests arrived, the host would greet everyone at the door. The older guests would sit farther from the door and the host would sit near the door. When it was time to serve the meal, the host would spread a *sofreh*, a long handmade piece of cloth, on the floor and set out the plates and bowls.

Then came the food—slices of fresh bread; plates full of cilantro, basil, green onion, mint, radishes, and the like; cheese; small bowls of pickles; and different types of yogurt mixtures. That was followed by big platters of rice topped with saffron, plates of chicken and meat, and bowls of soups and *ash*—thick soups usually made with meat and beans. Dessert was served at the same time as the rest of the meal—melons and *halva*, a type of sesame candy. Guests would wait for the oldest person to start eating, then everyone would follow. Leftovers were usually given to the poor.

As time passed, dining tables found their way into Persian households. Many Iranian women started working out of the house and just didn't have the time to cook all day. Remember, in the old days serving a chicken meant first going out in the yard to catch one, then slaughtering and cleaning it. Now it means going to the supermarket—or pulling one out of the freezer. Persian women buy dried herbs and canned goods in the market. Even the slow-cooked golden onions used in many dishes can be bought precooked.

That being said, there are certain cooking methods and recipes that just don't change, because they have been passed down through generations. Persian dishes still taste as good as years ago when it took many more hours to make them. Rice is still made the same way, kabobs are still mostly cooked on charcoal. Many festive traditions, like serving fish with herbed rice for *Norooz* (Persian New Year), remain.

In recent years Persian food has become more diverse. Foreign and regional foods have increased in popularity, making the taste and flavor of the cuisine as exciting as ever. Really, all you need to make good Persian food is love and a pinch of saffron.

A FEAST OF FLAVORS

Persian food cannot be described in a few words, because of its diversity. Every part of the country has its own techniques, flavors, and local ingredients. For example, there are some herbs like *khalvash* that can only be found in the northern part of the country, where locals use them in their stews and ash and as seasonings for chicken. In the south of Iran, everyday cooking is influenced by Arab and Indian cuisines. These bolder flavors include tamarind and cayenne pepper.

Persian cuisine is mild compared to some of its neighbors, and is about every ingredient being used to perfection. The order in which you add things is very important. When you are making Split Chickpea Stew (Khoresh-e-Gheimeh) on page 96, for example, that splash of rosewater has to be added at the very end or else its flavor is cooked away.

Persians love to make lamb and chicken kabobs on a charcoal barbecue because it gives such nice smokiness to the meat. Charcoal barbecues are mostly used on weekends or when people go camping.

Persian cuisine is also based on moderation and is very economical. Rice is used as a base for many meals, and red meat is added in small amounts. For example, a typical stew for 15 people might contain only 1½ pounds of lamb. Vegetables, herbs, and spices bulk up main dishes, and sides of salad or yogurt and mint help to extend the meal.

Home cooking and haute cuisine are essentially the same in Persian cooking. Really, the only difference is in the quality of the ingredients—the cut of meat or the grade of saffron.

Persian dishes can be divided into a few broad categories, based on their main ingredients and what part they play in the meal.

- **Starters and small plates:** Yogurt is an important part of many starters. It can be mixed with different types of vegetables and herbs, then served with some bread. Light salads are also served as starters in Persian cuisine, such as Cucumber & Tomato Salad (Salad Shirazi) on page 40.

- **Kookoos and egg dishes:** Very similar to Spanish frittatas, kookoos are common in Persian cuisine. They are egg-based and can be made with added meat, vegetables, or both. Kookoo is a great choice for a light dinner.

- **Soups:** These can be served as starters, especially at parties and gatherings, or as a light meals with bread and salad.

- **Ash:** Basically a thicker version of soup, ash usually includes rice and substantial amounts of beans and meat, which make it a meal. In my family, we prefer lamb over beef because it is more tender and flavorful—but that's a matter of personal taste.

Garmi and Sardi—
Hot and Cold

Ancient Persian medicine classifies food into two groups: *garmi* (hot or heating) and *sardi* (cold or cooling). These foods are not literally hot or cold, but affect the body in different ways. Hot or garmi foods are rich and calorie-heavy, and oily or very sweet or spicy. They thicken the blood and speed metabolism. Cold or sardi foods are light and fresh tasting. They dilute the blood and slow metabolism. These classifications were developed by traditional healers more than a thousand years ago and mirror similar concepts in traditional Chinese medicine and Ayurveda, which suggest that an imbalance of hot and cold leads to illness.

Some examples of garmi foods are beets, garlic, celery, lamb, organic chicken, honey, cinnamon, jams, mint (dried and fresh), melons, figs (dried and fresh), bananas, dates, raisins, peanuts, walnuts, cashews, sesame oil, saffron, and ginger.

Some examples of sardi foods are eggplant, zucchini, barley, potato, corn, pumpkin, lettuce, green beans, strawberries, apricots, kiwis, rice, fish, non-organic chicken, sumac, and yogurt.

People may also be said to have a hot or cold nature; those with a hot temperament eat more sardi foods to balance them out, and vice versa. Balancing garmi and sardi foods in preparing dishes and arranging meals makes for a symmetry in aesthetics and taste that is essential to good Persian cuisine.

For example, Pomegranate & Walnut Stew (Khoresh-e-Fesenjan) on page 87 has walnuts, which are garmi, so we add some cooked mashed pumpkin to balance it, because pumpkin is sardi. When we make Yogurt & Spinach (Borani Esfenaj) on page 33, we add some garlic and pepper (garmi) to balance the sardi spinach and yogurt.

- **Khoresh:** In Persian cuisine, Khoresh, or stews, are considered main courses and can be served with plain steamed white rice or Herbs & Rice (Sabzi Polo) on page 106.

- **Rice:** One of the most important parts of just about any Persian meal is long-grain white rice. Making plain steamed white rice (*chelo*) is a key skill in Persian cuisine, as it is the go-to accompaniment for many stews and other dishes. An easier way to make plain rice is by employing a technique called *kateh*, or boiling it in water until it's completely cooked.

- **Polo:** This is my favorite category of Persian cuisine, because it encompasses my all-time favorite dish, Green Beans & Beef Mixed Rice (Loobia Polo) on page 165. Basically, every *polo* is made the same way: cook some rice halfway through, layer it in a pot with a cooked filling, and let everything steam together. One method yields endless possibilities. Polo can be made with only herbs or a combination of herbs and chicken, lamb, beef, or even shrimp.

- **Koofteh:** These are meatballs made with various seasonal ingredients. *Kooftehs* have different flavors, from semi-sweet to tart to sour, depending on the ingredients and spices used. They are easy dishes that come together in very little time.

- **Kabobs:** One of the most popular Persian specialties, kabobs are made from lamb, beef, or chicken—sometimes chunks and sometimes ground. Families usually make them on a small barbecue grill on weekends or when they are on a picnic.

- **Drinks:** Tea for we Iranians is like coffee for many Americans. But drinks are not limited only to tea. Persian flavored syrups make wonderful drinks when they are mixed with water and ice.

- **Desserts and sweet treats:** There are sweets made with dates and others made with honey, coconut, or different flours, full of beautiful aromas and the tastes of saffron, cardamom, and rosewater. Some are served on specific occasions. For example, *halva*, a very dense pudding made of flour and saffron syrup, is usually served at funerals, and *Kaachi*, which is the same as halva but not as dense, is served to a woman who has recently had a baby.

THE PERSIAN KITCHEN

Most of the fruit, vegetables, grains, and other ingredients used in Persian cooking are grown in Iran. For instance, rice and tea is grown in the north, some parts of the south and southwest are famous for dates, and a very large portion of the world's saffron is grown in Khorasan in northwestern Iran.

Iranians tend to cook with seasonal produce and buy ingredients and products daily from markets. My maman went out in the morning two or three times a week to buy items she needed for our meals. My sister-in-law's uncles had a farm near Tehran where they grew delicious organic eggplants, cauliflower, carrots, and cabbage. My maman would fry the eggplants and freeze them, then make pickles with the cauliflower, carrots, and cabbage.

Though fresh is always better, in some recipes canned produce will save a lot of time, and sometimes using frozen produce instead of fresh (if something is not in season) will not make a big difference in taste.

Because rice, lentils, beans, and some other dry ingredients are used so often in the Persian kitchen, we buy them in bulk. I remember my baba always bought huge bags of rice for the family that would last for about six months, kept in a cool, dark place.

There are no substitutes for many of the spices and flavorings in Persian food. That's why I suggest that you stock up on the staples that you will use frequently. Some will be very familiar, like rice and cinnamon and yogurt, and others may be a little less familiar. Find a Persian food store in your area; Middle Eastern, Arab, Turkish, and even Indian stores will also have most of the ingredients you need. The most important Persian ingredients are not difficult to find. There are some online stores where you can order anything you can't buy locally (you'll find a few listed in the Resources section on page 219). It's always a good idea to store spices in small glass jars or other airtight containers away from sunlight.

Persian Pantry Staples

- **Rice (berenj)** برنج This is the most important grain of Persian cuisine. Persian dishes use long-grain white rice; when cooked, the grains remain separate. Basmati rice is a good choice.

- **Saffron (zaferan)** زعفران These delicate threads, harvested from the inner parts of crocus flowers, are used in both savory and sweet Persian foods. The best saffron comes from Khorasan in northeastern Iran, cultivated by people who have been planting flowers for generations. Always buy saffron in threads and not ground, as processed versions might be mixed with turmeric, cayenne, and other orange and red spices.

- **Turmeric (zardchoobeh)** زردچوبه This ground spice is used regularly in Persian cuisine, both for its color and its health benefits. Because it has a strong taste, turmeric is used in very small quantities.

- **Cinnamon (darchin)** دارچین This is a familiar spice in many cuisines, used in both sweet and savory dishes. I opt for ground cinnamon in cooking but keep a few sticks on hand for special dishes. For example, Persians sometimes brew their tea with a stick of cinnamon for a touch of sweetness.

- **Cardamom (hel)** هل Whole cardamom pods and ground cardamom are mainstays of Persian cuisine. However, I stock only the whole pods in my kitchen and grind them myself using a mortar and pestle, as freshly ground cardamom has a stronger taste. You can brew two cardamom pods with black tea to give it a nice infusion.

- **Sumac (somagh)** سماق This spice comes from the berries of the sumac bush and is usually sold dried and ground into a coarse powder, which is how it's used in Persian cuisine. It has a tart, tangy, sour taste, a bit like lemon, that goes really well with different types of kabobs.

- **Barberries (zereshk)** زرشک These small dried berries are sweet and sour. Their bright color and sharp flavor add a wonderful accent to many rice and egg dishes.

- **Cayenne (felfel ghrmez)** فلفل قرمز Every dish needs a little bit of heat, but not too much. A small dash of ground cayenne pepper is used in mixed rice dishes to amp up the color and flavor.

- **Rosewater (golab)** گلاب My favorite seasoning and a must-have in any Persian pantry. Rosewater is made through the steam distillation of rose petals. It is used in some stews, and also in sweets, pastries, halvas, and even drinks. A tablespoon of good rosewater is enough to elevate a dish. Make sure to check the ingredient list on the bottle; rosewater should be the only thing listed.

- **Garlic (seer) سیر** Garlic is used frequently in the Persian kitchen in its whole, minced, and powdered forms. Have some fresh and powdered on hand at all times (fresh garlic keeps for a long time in the refrigerator). This pungent allium is used most often in the north of Iran, in local dishes such as Mirza Ghasemi (Smoky Eggplant & Eggs) on page 55.

- **Mint (Na'naa) نعناع** This aromatic herb is used fresh or dried in the Persian kitchen, added to stews and salads and also stirred into yogurt. An assortment of chopped fresh mint, chives, parsley, and dill makes a great topping for almost any Persian dish.

- **Tomato paste (robb-e-gojeh farangi) رب گوجه فرنگی** Tomatoes were not a part of ancient Persian cuisine, and when they entered the Persian kitchen, tomato paste was the most common form. It has a strong taste and is therefore used in small quantities, mainly in mixed rice dishes and stews. In some recipes, tomato sauce can be substituted.

- **Dried lime (limoo amani) لیمو عمانی** These have a stronger taste than fresh limes and very hard skin, so they need to simmer for some time to soften. Dried lime tastes like lime with a hint of vinegar and a hint of sweetness; it's a bright, fresh flavor. In some dishes you can substitute fresh lime, but it's best to have some dried lime on hand because the taste is distinctive. Dried limes come whole and as a powder. Whole is preferable, but if you can only find the powder, use 1 teaspoon of powdered lime in place of one whole dried lime. You don't eat the whole ones. Just spoon the dish up around them, or pick the limes out right before serving.

- **Yogurt (mast) ماست** Many Persian side dishes and appetizers include yogurt as their main ingredient, and at dinnertime there is usually one small bowl of yogurt, cucumber, and mint at each place setting. In the old days, Iranians preferred full-fat yogurt, but these days families use low-fat yogurt too. The yogurt used in Persian cuisine is usually thick—so plain Greek yogurt would be a great choice.

- **Nuts آجیل** We love nuts, including pistachios, walnuts, hazelnuts, peanuts, cashews, and almonds. Many people love them plain, but you can also season them with salt or other flavorings. My baba's family had almond and hazelnut trees in their yard, and I just couldn't wait to climb the trees and pick some good nuts whenever we visited them.

- **Dried fruit** میوه خشک Dried fruits are integral parts of Persian food culture and can be found in almost every Iranian household. Raisins, dates, dried figs, and dried apricots are some of the most used dried fruits in Iran, especially during Persian New Year—Norooz.

Persian cuisine is based on seasonal and fresh products. If there is one thing to remember about Persian staples, it's to always, always buy fresh ingredients, which is a main reason why the food doesn't need much seasoning to hold on to its flavors. Start fresh and you can store all these spices and staples (including rice, beans, and lentils) longer.

Always buy whole saffron threads and grind them yourself, using a mortar and pestle. Add ¼ teaspoon sugar and ¼ teaspoon salt for every five saffron threads for easier grinding.

I buy ground cinnamon, turmeric, cayenne, and garlic powder because these spices don't lose their aroma and can be stored for a long time. For the rest, including black pepper, cardamom, and saffron, grind the whole spices yourself. You can use a mortar and pestle or a small coffee grinder. Buy a separate coffee grinder just for spices, because you don't want any coffee flavor in your seasonings, and vice versa. You'll also need a separate tool—preferably a mortar and pestle—that is used only for saffron. It might seem like a lot of work to grind your own spices, but there is a huge difference between freshly ground spice and previously ground spice.

How to Prep Persian Ingredients

There are some ingredients in Persian cuisine that need to be prepped before you add them to a recipe. Once you master these simple methods, outlined below, you'll be ready to tackle every recipe in this book.

SAFFRON

Since the whole threads will not dissolve into foods during the cooking process, saffron must be either bloomed or ground ahead of time. I always bloom a small amount of saffron at the beginning of the week and keep it in a jar in the refrigerator for five to seven days. In Persian cooking, saffron is mostly used to garnish plain white rice or to add flavor to stews and mixed rice dishes.

To grind saffron, put 4 or 5 saffron threads, ¼ teaspoon sugar, and ¼ teaspoon salt in a mortar. (The sugar and salt make the grinding process easier.) Grind the mixture with the pestle until it is completely ground and resembles fine sugar. It's always better to grind saffron right before using it to keep the aroma and taste fresh.

There are two ways to bloom saffron, and both will yield equally satisfying results. The following instructions will give you enough bloomed saffron to make three or four recipes in this book.

- **Ice:** Place two ice cubes in a small bowl and sprinkle ¼ teaspoon ground saffron over the top. Let it sit at room temperature until the ice is fully melted.

- **Hot water:** Place ¼ teaspoon ground saffron in a small, heatproof bowl and pour in ⅓ cup hot water. Cover the bowl with a piece of cloth and let it sit at room temperature until the saffron is fully dissolved.

BASIC SYRUP

Basic or simple syrup is used in various sweet dishes and desserts. Combine equal amounts of sugar and water in a saucepan and bring the mixture to a boil. Simmer uncovered for 15 minutes, until the sugar is completely dissolved and the syrup thickens a little. Store the syrup in a jar in the refrigerator.

GOLDEN FRIED ONIONS

Golden fried onions are used to decorate food or add extra flavor to a dish. Peel and thinly slice some onions, drop them in boiling water, and drain them after 1 minute. Pat the onion slices dry with a kitchen towel, then panfry them in hot oil until they are completely golden brown, 7 to 8 minutes. Drain the onions in a stainless steel colander. You can store these golden fried onions for up to 10 days in an airtight container at room temperature.

POMEGRANATES

To deseed a pomegranate, use a sharp paring knife to remove the crown on top, without cutting through the seeds. Then cut the pomegranate in half through the equator. You should see the seeds laid out in each half like a five-pointed star, separated by white membranes. Hold each half in your hand with your thumbs on the cut side and your other fingers on the top, and gently pull back the skin to loosen the seeds. Hold one half over a bowl with the cut-side facing your palm. Spread your fingers out so the seeds can fall through them. Using the back of

How to Make
Easy Persian Rice (Kateh)

Kateh is fluffy, cooked white rice that has separated grains. This is the kind of family-style rice that we use for stews and mixed rice dishes. (Steamed Persian rice, called *chelo*, is a style of rice served at gatherings and parties.) Kateh is made with a crispy golden crust called *tahdig*—which many consider to be the best part. To make kateh, or any other type of Persian-style rice, you need long-grain white rice such as basmati. Kateh takes about 45 minutes of cooking, and this recipe serves four people.

2 cups long-grain white rice, such as basmati, rinsed and drained

4 to 5 cups cold water

⅓ cup vegetable oil

1 teaspoon salt

1. Combine the rice and water in a large pot over high heat. The water should come up about ½ inch above the rice. Bring the liquid to a boil, then cook uncovered until the rice is tender and the water has almost completely evaporated, about 20 minutes.

2. Using a fork, push the rice grains from the sides to the middle of the pot, then pour the vegetable oil around the outer edges. Cover the pot, reduce the heat to medium high, and cook for 10 minutes. The crispy tahdig will start to form around the edges and at the bottom of the pot. Turn the heat to very low and cook for another 15 minutes. Stir in the salt.

3. Place a large plate on top of the pot and carefully turn the pot over so the rice falls onto the plate, crispy crust–side up.

a wooden spoon, give the pomegranate a couple of good whacks to dislodge the seeds. Whack around the sides as well to get all the seeds out. Repeat with the other half.

RICE

To prepare white rice for cooking, put the rice in a fine-mesh colander set inside a large bowl. Fill the bowl with enough cold running water to cover the rice. Using your fingers, mix the rice and water for a few seconds, then lift the colander and discard the water. Repeat this process four times. You can also let the rice soak in water for a couple of hours and then rinse it.

Essential Equipment

There are a few tools you'll need to make the recipes in this book, but the good news is that they're easy to find, and chances are you already have many of them in your kitchen. Here are the absolute must-haves:

- **Box grater:** Many Persian dishes call for grating onions and other vegetables. A box grater is stable and easy to work with, and most models offer three types of holes, plus a side that slices. For the recipes in this book, use the largest holes on your box grater.

- **Colander:** To make polo and chelo you'll need a colander to strain the rice, as it will be cooked halfway and then cooked again with or without fillings. Buy a fine-mesh one so you can also use it to wash your rice.

- **Kettle and teapot:** Brewing Persian-style tea requires both a kettle for boiling the water and a teapot for brewing the tea—and preferably a small piece of cloth, too. (The cloth is used to cover the teapot while the tea is brewing. This helps the tea to brew evenly and stay hot.)

- **Ladle:** For all the soup, ash, and stew you'll be making, you'll need a good ladle so you can serve food easily.

- **Mortar and pestle:** As I mentioned before, saffron is the star of the Persian kitchen, so having a mortar and pestle to grind it with is a must.

- **Nonstick frying pan:** Get a nice big one, so you'll have plenty of room to sauté and fry all kinds of ingredients.

- **Nonstick rice pot:** You'll need this to ensure that the tahdig browns just right when you're making Polo and Chelo. Try to find a pot that holds more rice than you typically make for your family, so you can also use it when you have more people over.

- **Spice or coffee grinder:** This will be for your other spices—because saffron needs a grinder all its own. Of course, a second mortar and pestle would do the trick, too, but an electric grinder will save you time and effort.

Nice to Have

- **Charcoal barbecue:** Persians love the smoky flavor that charcoal grilling imparts to kabobs and vegetables (especially eggplant). A very small portable grill is all you'll need.

- **Food processor:** If grating vegetables on a box grater seems like a lot of work, a food processor will make the job much quicker. You can also use it for slicing and to purée cooked potatoes and eggplant.

- **Rice cooker:** If you're new to cooking rice, this handy appliance will make your life easier, as it does everything automatically and doesn't require you to monitor the process or do anything.

TIPS AND TRICKS TO MAKE PERSIAN COOKING EASIER

Persian cooking is easy; it only requires that the ingredients be mixed and added in the right sequence at the right time. It does require attention, though, and sometimes speed. That's why *mise en place* is very important in Persian cooking. Mise en place is a French term that means the ingredients are measured, washed (if needed), prepped, and within arm's reach before you start cooking. If you have all your ingredients ready to go, you'll be able to make any of the recipes in this book with confidence, as the steps are all pretty basic.

In Iran, the majority of people use gas stoves rather than electric stoves. Food cooks more quickly on gas stoves, so if you are using an electric stove, you may have to add some extra cooking time, depending on the recipe.

The recipes that require you to pay particularly close attention to cooking time are the mixed rice dishes, or polo. They have four parts: (1) cooking the filling; (2) parboiling the rice (the center of the grain will still be hard); (3) layering the rice and the filling in a pot; and (4) steaming the whole thing.

To steam the polo, we pour some water around the edges of the pot and poke five holes in the layers of rice. This will help the steam escape and prevent the rice from sticking to the bottom of the pot. The water starts steaming, and the parboiled rice is fully cooked with this steam. Over low heat, it usually takes 15 minutes for the rice to start steaming and then another 15 minutes for the polo to cook completely. But that may vary based on the quality of the rice and also on your stove.

The steaming time for polos can also vary between 30 minutes and 1 hour, based on whether you're steaming the rice over medium or medium-low heat. Iranian women usually cook polos longer over very low heat; they want to keep them warm for when everyone comes home, since these types of dishes burn on the bottom when reheated. However, oversteaming rice can result in a much less flavorful finished dish. For your first few polos, follow the recipes in this book as they are written, checking the rice at each stage. After you make a few, you'll have a good sense of how long to cook them on your stove, with your rice, and to your taste.

Here are a few more tips:

- Many recipes don't remind you to rinse the rice first; they just assume you'll do it. Always wash the rice four times before you start cooking to get rid of excess starch and other impurities. (See page 23 for rinsing instructions.)

- Having some bloomed saffron on hand goes a long way. I always have a small jar in the refrigerator; it keeps for about a week. This saves time in cooking and it's always ready to use. (See page 21 for instructions on blooming saffron.)

- Many recipes for Persian dishes start with "sauté the onions." This does not mean sauté until translucent—it means sauté until the onion is golden brown, which takes more time. Many Iranian women cook up large batches of onions on the weekend to use throughout the week.

- Use canned beans. Different types of beans are used frequently in Persian cooking, and for some recipes, using canned beans and chickpeas saves lots of time without sacrificing flavor. When using canned beans, add them at the end of cooking so they absorb the flavor of the dish without breaking down.

Nush-e Joon!

Persian food is all about sharing with your loved ones. For that reason, food is served in a special way. Polo, chelo, and mixed rice is served on large platters, and stews are served in shallow plates the size of a pie pan that can be shared among three or four people. There is usually a big platter for tahdig, too, but my maman always had to distribute these crispy pieces of crust herself to prevent my brother and I from fighting over them! Soup and ash are served in big bowls that can be shared by everyone at the table, and there is always some bread (usually lavash) on the table too.

Tahdig, the layer of golden crunchy potato or rice crust at the bottom of a pot of stew, is so delicious that everyone wants to have the first piece—and the last!

The kitchen is the heart of every Iranian household, where magic happens by mixing saffron and rosewater or brewing some Persian tea. Even the sound of rice grains being measured for the next meal is special to me. The kitchen is where I figured out how much I love my life, my family, and cooking. Each recipe in this book is a love letter to my native cuisine and a nod to all the Persian home cooks who came before me.

Nush-e joon literally translates to "May it be a pleasure to your soul." We say it when we come to the table, meaning enjoy your meal—love this food that brings you life. May all these recipes bring nothing but happiness to your soul and your kitchen!

About the Recipes

As you cook your way through this book, you'll find several icons attached to each recipe. Here's what they mean:

VEGETARIAN no meat or fish, but there may be dairy, eggs, or honey

VEGAN no meat, fish, dairy, eggs, or honey

QUICK & EASY can be prepared and served in 30 minutes or less

WORTH THE WAIT requires more than 1 hour to make (a lot of which is often passive cooking time)

Each dish also has a level of difficulty scale from one to four stars. But please don't be put off: The four-star recipes just have a few more steps and require a bit more patience.

These recipes are extremely easy and use ingredients you're likely to have at hand. The steps usually include mixing the ingredients in a bowl, then employing a basic cooking technique such as sautéing. No special knowledge is needed, and you won't spend a lot of time in the kitchen.

These recipes usually require a bit more advance preparation. For example, the meat has to be marinated, or the kookoos (frittatas) have to be mixed in a bowl and then cooked individually. They usually take a bit more time.

These recipes are slightly more difficult and have more ingredients. They require more cooking techniques and time spent in the kitchen. Most of the mixed rice dishes have three stars, but once you make them a couple of times, they get easier.

These recipes have more involved steps and a longer lists of ingredients. For example, when making Tabrizi Meatballs (page 136), it's very important to ensure that the meatballs do not fall apart as they are cooking in the sauce.

2 APPETIZERS & SNACKS

YOGURT & CUCUMBER

—————————— ماست و خيار MAST-O-KHIAR ——————————

Serves 4
Prep: 10 minutes

2 Persian cucumbers or any
seedless cucumbers

3 cups plain Greek yogurt

3 tablespoons chopped
walnuts, divided

2 tablespoons raisins, divided

½ teaspoon salt

1 tablespoon dried mint,
plus more for garnish

VEGETARIAN, QUICK & EASY Mast-o-Khiar is one of the
most basic appetizers in Persian cuisine. In its simplest form, it's a seasoned yogurt with small chunks of
cucumber and some salt; from there you can dress it
up with add-ins like nuts, dried fruit, and your favorite
spices. In my family we add dried mint, walnuts, and
raisins, which give the appetizer a very nice flavor and
mix of textures. Serve this at the beginning of a meal,
either in small individual bowls or in one large bowl,
and pass bread for dipping and slathering.

1. Cut the cucumbers into quarters lengthwise, then chop
them into very small pieces.

2. In a large bowl, mix together the chopped cucumber, yogurt,
2 tablespoons of chopped walnuts, 1 tablespoon of raisins, the
salt, and the dried mint.

3. Garnish with the remaining 1 tablespoon of walnuts and
1 tablespoon of raisins and some more dried mint.

4. Serve immediately.

INGREDIENT TIP When buying dried mint, the lighter
the color, the better the quality. You can also use chopped
fresh mint instead of dried mint.

YOGURT & EGGPLANT

بورانی بادمجان BORANI BADEMJAAN

Serves 4
Prep: 15 minutes,
plus 20 minutes
for chilling
Cook: 30 minutes

Nonstick cooking spray

2 large eggplants

1 tablespoon olive oil

1 onion, thinly sliced

2 garlic cloves, minced

3 cups plain Greek yogurt

½ teaspoon salt

½ teaspoon freshly ground
black pepper

VEGETARIAN Borani Bademjaan can be a full meal on its own if it's paired with some warm bread. The combination of roasted eggplant and yogurt with the garlic and caramelized onions makes the best dip for any occasion. (If you don't have fresh garlic on hand, you can substitute 2 teaspoons of garlic powder and add it with salt and pepper at the end.) The longer this dip cools in the fridge, the more delicious it will be.

1. Preheat the oven to 425°F. Line a baking sheet with aluminum foil and coat it with nonstick cooking spray.

2. Pierce the eggplants a few times with a fork. Place them on the prepared baking sheet and roast them in the oven for 30 minutes or until they are fully cooked and the skin is wrinkled. Remove the eggplants from the oven and let them cool completely.

3. As the eggplants are roasting, heat the olive oil in a medium skillet over medium heat and cook the onion and garlic until they are tender and golden brown, about 10 minutes.

4. Peel the eggplants and chop them very finely.

5. In a large bowl, mix together the chopped eggplant, caramelized onion and garlic, yogurt, salt, and pepper.

6. Cover the bowl and let the mixture chill in the refrigerator for 20 to 30 minutes before serving.

BEYOND THE BASICS Use a charcoal or gas grill to give a nice, smoky, Persian taste to the eggplants.

YOGURT & ZUCCHINI
ماست و کدو MAST-O-KADOO

Serves 4
Prep: 10 minutes,
plus 20 minutes
for chilling

2 zucchini

2 cups plain Greek yogurt

¼ teaspoon salt

¼ teaspoon freshly ground
black pepper

½ teaspoon garlic powder

1 tablespoon chopped
fresh mint

VEGETARIAN, QUICK & EASY We used to have Mast-o-Kadoo almost every day in the summertime, when our family garden was overflowing with zucchini. Not only is it a refreshing dip for bread and crackers, but it's also great for people who suffer from heart health issues, as some scientific research suggests that zucchini may help regulate blood pressure.

1. Grate the zucchini. Squeeze it well in a clean kitchen towel or place it in a fine-mesh colander and press on it with the back of a wooden spoon. Discard the excess water.

2. In a separate bowl, mix together the grated zucchini, yogurt, salt, pepper, garlic powder, and mint.

3. Cover the bowl and let the mixture chill in the refrigerator for 20 to 30 minutes before serving.

SUBSTITUTION TIP You can substitute dried mint if you'd like, though it will impart a milder flavor.

YOGURT & SPINACH

بورانی اسفناج BORANI ESFENAJ

Serves 4
Prep: 10 minutes,
plus 20 minutes
for chilling
Cook: 5 minutes

1 (6-ounce) bag baby spinach,
roughly chopped

2 garlic cloves, minced

2 cups plain Greek yogurt,
plus 1 tablespoon, divided

½ teaspoon salt

1 teaspoon freshly ground
black pepper

1 teaspoon bloomed
saffron (see page 21)

VEGETARIAN Borani Esfenaj is basically the Persian
equivalent of creamy spinach dip, infused with lots
of spicy black pepper and heady saffron flavor. If
you're sensitive to heat, feel free to cut back a bit
on the black pepper.

1. Heat a large, dry skillet over medium heat.

2. Sauté the spinach for 3 to 4 minutes or until it is tender
and wilted. Add the garlic and cook for another minute. Remove
the skillet from the heat and let the spinach and garlic cool.

3. In a large bowl, mix together the spinach and garlic, 2 cups
of yogurt, the salt, and black pepper.

4. In a small bowl, whisk together the remaining 1 tablespoon
of yogurt and the bloomed saffron.

5. Drizzle the saffron-yogurt mixture over the Borani Esfenaj,
then cover the bowl and chill the dip in the refrigerator for
20 to 30 minutes before serving.

INGREDIENT TIP A whole bag of baby spinach will look
like a lot when you chop it up fresh, but don't worry, it will
wilt down quite a bit during cooking.

YOGURT & BEETS

بورانی لبو BORANI LABOO

Serves 4
Prep: 5 minutes,
plus 20 minutes
for chilling
Cook: 45 minutes

2 large red beets

1 garlic clove, minced

2 cups plus 1 tablespoon plain Greek yogurt

½ teaspoon salt

VEGETARIAN Borani Laboo is one of the most beautiful and flavorful Persian appetizers. Its naturally bold-pink color stands out on any table, and its sweet-tangy-garlicky flavor is delicious on bread, crackers, or by itself, eaten with a spoon. If the beets are not sweet enough for your taste, add 1 tablespoon of white sugar to the dip.

1. In a medium saucepan of water brought to a boil over high heat, add the beets and boil them until they are fork tender, about 45 minutes. Drain the beets and set them aside to cool.

2. When the beets are cool enough to handle, peel them, cut them into chunks, and either purée them in a food processor or mash them in a large bowl with a potato masher.

3. If you used a food processor, transfer the puréed beets to a large bowl. Add the garlic, yogurt, and salt and mix well.

4. Cover the bowl and let the mixture chill in the refrigerator for 20 to 30 minutes before serving.

MAKE IT EASIER If you're short on time, use canned beets instead of fresh.

YOGURT & DILL

Serves 4
Prep: 5 minutes,
plus 20 minutes
for chilling

3 tablespoons chopped
fresh dill

2 cups plain Greek yogurt

½ teaspoon freshly ground
black pepper

VEGETARIAN, QUICK & EASY Mast-o-Shevid has a very fresh taste, thanks to the dill. It pairs well with mixed rice dishes such as Black-Eyed Peas & Beef Mixed Rice (Loobia Cheshm Bolboli Polo) page 170. And as an added bonus, it is thought to help balance cholesterol and blood pressure.

1. In a large bowl, mix together the dill, yogurt, and pepper.

2. Chill in the refrigerator for 20 to 30 minutes before serving.

COOKING TIP My maman used to add some shredded zucchini and dried mint to this dip for more texture and flavor.

CHEESE, HERB & BREAD BALLS

— دویماج DOYMAJ —

Serves 4
Prep: 10 minutes,
plus 30 minutes
for chilling
Cook: 12 minutes

4 large flour tortillas,
cut into small pieces

1 cup crumbled feta cheese

1 cup chopped walnuts

½ cup chopped fresh basil

½ cup chopped fresh mint

2 to 3 tablespoons unsalted
butter, melted

¼ to ½ cup water, as needed

MAKE IT EASIER The
traditional way to make
doymaj is by mixing the
ingredients with your hands,
but you can use a food processor instead if you like.

COOKING TIP Instead
of water, some families
add heavy cream to moisten
the doymaj. For this recipe,
1 to 2 tablespoons of heavy
cream should do the trick.

VEGETARIAN Doymaj is homemade deliciousness from Tabriz. It is basically a mixture of dried thin bread, cheese, herbs, walnut, and butter. The basil and mint are optional—some families add them and some don't. It's usually made in big batches for family gatherings and is served with watermelon or cantaloupe on hot summer days. In the summertime, many Persians enjoy Doymaj as a lighter, full meal.

1. Preheat the oven to 400°F. Line a baking sheet with parchment paper.

2. Spread the tortilla pieces on the prepared baking sheet and bake them until they are dry and crispy, about 12 minutes. Remove them from the oven, let them cool slightly, then crush them with a rolling pin.

3. In a large bowl, mix together the crushed tortillas, feta cheese, walnuts, basil, mint, and melted butter, using your hands.

4. If the mixture seems too dry to be rolled into balls, add some water, a little bit at a time, mixing after each addition until the mixture is sticky.

5. Shape the mixture into 2-inch balls and place them on a baking sheet. Chill the balls in the refrigerator for 30 minutes before serving.

My Memories

Doymaj is filling, healthy, and very delicious. That makes it a great choice for Iftar (the evening meal when we break the day-time fast during Ramadan), since each small bite is nutritious and not difficult to digest. Iftar is, of course, different in every family; some enjoy a full meal and others, like my family, have more of a brunch-type meal of fresh fruits and vegetables, bread and cheese, and sweets.

Sharing your food with family, friends, neighbors, and the poor is strongly advised during Ramadan

Since Muslims do not eat or drink from sunrise to sunset every day during Ramadan, it's especially important that, when we break the fast, we eat food that is nutritious and will keep us full for a long time. Fruit, vegetables, and complex carbs like beans and whole grains are good choices. It's best to avoid deep-fried food and creamy and very sweet dishes, as they fill you up but don't offer much nutrition.

In my family, for Suhoor (the meal before sunrise) we eat a meal full of protein and complex carbs, such as lentil soup, chicken breast, or beans. For Iftar, we start with dates and a light soup like Vermicelli Soup (Soope Reshteh) on page 67, then some cheese and bread, like Doymaj, and of course, tea. It's good to pause after a few bites so the body can handle the food after fasting all day. We always end the meal with something naturally sweet such as honey, dates, and fresh fruit.

Sharing your food with family, friends, neighbors, and the poor is strongly advised during Ramadan, as you never know who around you might not be able to afford to buy food or is not able to cook or eat a good meal. Ramadan is all about sharing what you have with everyone.

EGGPLANT DIP

کشک بادمجان KASHK-E-BADEMJAAN

Serves 4
Prep: 10 minutes
Cook: 50 minutes

6 tablespoons vegetable oil, divided

4 eggplants, peeled and cut into small pieces

2 onions, 1 chopped and 1 sliced, divided

2 garlic cloves, minced, divided

½ teaspoon ground turmeric

½ teaspoon freshly ground black pepper

¼ cup water

¾ cup plus 1 tablespoon kashk (yogurt whey, see page 39)

1 tablespoon dried mint, divided

1 teaspoon bloomed saffron (see page 21)

VEGETARIAN Kashk-e-Bedemjaan is a mixture of *Bademjaan* (eggplant) and *kashk* (a type of yogurt whey). You can find kashk in the refrigerated section of Middle Eastern stores. They are usually sold in medium-sized glass jars. This dish has a salty, garlicky flavor, and is perfect served with some warm bread and topped with fresh herbs such as basil. It can also be served as a light main dish.

1. Heat 2 tablespoons of olive oil in a large skillet over medium heat. Add the eggplant and cook for 10 minutes, stirring frequently, until golden brown on all sides. Transfer the eggplant to a plate and set it aside.

2. Heat 1 tablespoon of oil in the same skillet over medium heat. Sauté the chopped onion and 1 minced garlic clove until golden brown, about 10 minutes. Add the turmeric, black pepper, eggplant, and water. Cover the skillet and let the vegetables cook for 10 minutes.

3. Turn off the heat and mash the eggplant mixture using a potato masher, or transfer the mixture to a food processor and purée until smooth. Transfer the mashed or puréed mixture back to the skillet.

4. Mix in the kashk, half of the dried mint, and the bloomed saffron. Place the skillet over medium heat and stir for 5 minutes until everything is fully incorporated.

5. Heat 2 tablespoons of oil in a separate skillet over medium heat and sauté the sliced onion for 10 minutes until soft and golden brown. Remove the skillet from the heat and set it aside.

6. In a small skillet, heat the remaining 1 tablespoon of oil over medium heat and sauté the remaining minced garlic clove until golden, 2 to 3 minutes. Transfer the cooked garlic to a plate, add the remaining dried mint to the same skillet, and sauté for 30 seconds or until aromatic.

7. Serve the eggplant dip in a shallow dish topped with the caramelized onion, sautéed garlic, and sautéed dried mint.

COOKING TIP Frying eggplants requires using a lot of oil. That's why we cook them halfway and then complete the cooking with a little water. You can also cook the eggplants in the oven at 400°F for 25 minutes and follow the same recipe.

SUBSTITUTION TIP If you have trouble finding kashk, you can use full-fat Greek yogurt or labneh, which is a thick, Lebanese strained yogurt.

CUCUMBER & TOMATO SALAD

سالاد شیرازی SALAD SHIRAZI

Serves 4
Prep: 15 minutes,
plus 30 minutes
for chilling

3 Persian cucumbers, or
any seedless cucumbers,
finely chopped

1 small red onion,
finely chopped

2 large tomatoes,
finely chopped

4 tablespoons freshly
squeezed lemon juice

½ teaspoon salt

½ teaspoon freshly ground
black pepper

1 tablespoon dried mint

VEGAN, QUICK & EASY Salad Shirazi is one of those dishes that everyone makes. The ingredients are very common, and many countries have a salad that's similar. It is best served with Green Beans & Beef Mixed Rice (page 165). This salad is perfect for hot summer days.

1. In a large bowl, mix the cucumbers, onion, and tomatoes with the lemon juice, salt, and pepper.

2. Cover the bowl and refrigerate the salad for at least 30 minutes.

3. To serve, top with the dried mint and give it a nice stir.

INGREDIENT TIP Choose tomatoes that are firm and don't contain too much water, as they will release liquid when they are mixed with the other ingredients. Also, cutting firm tomatoes is easier. If the core of the tomato looks watery and has too many seeds, cut it out and discard it.

POTATOES & CARAMELIZED ONION

دو پیازه آلو DO PIAZEH ALOO

Serves 2
Prep: 5 minutes
Cook: 35 minutes

1 large white potato, peeled and cut into 1-inch cubes

2 tablespoons vegetable oil

2 yellow onions, chopped

2 tablespoons tomato paste

½ teaspoon salt

½ teaspoon freshly ground black pepper

½ teaspoon ground turmeric

VEGAN Do Piaze Aloo is a very simple dish from Shiraz, a city in southwestern Iran known for its warm-hearted people. Potato is called "aloo" by some Shirazi people, and onion is also "aloo," so the rule of this dish is *do* (two) onions for one *aloo* (potato). This dish can be served as an appetizer or a light dinner.

1. Bring a large pot of water to a boil over high heat, add the potatoes, and boil them for about 15 minutes or until they are fork tender. Drain and set the potatoes aside.

2. In a large skillet, heat the vegetable oil over medium heat and sauté the onions for about 10 minutes or until golden brown.

3. Add the tomato paste, salt, pepper, and turmeric to the skillet and sauté for 30 seconds or until the mixture is fragrant.

4. Add the potatoes to the skillet and mix well until everything is fully combined. Cover the skillet and cook for 5 to 10 minutes, until the potatoes are heated through.

5. Serve hot.

COOKING TIP If you like Do Piazeh Aloo spicier, add some cayenne pepper. You can also fry the potatoes in a separate pan and add them to the onions for a crispier dish.

STUFFED BELL PEPPERS

────────────── دلمه فلفل DOLMEH FELFEL ──────────────

Serves 4
Prep: 20 minutes
Cook: 1 hour

½ cup long-grain white rice, such as basmati, rinsed and drained

2½ to 3 cups water, divided

Pinch salt, plus ½ teaspoon

3 tablespoons vegetable oil, divided

1 yellow onion, finely chopped

2 garlic cloves, minced

½ pound lean ground beef

½ teaspoon cayenne pepper

½ teaspoon ground turmeric

2 tablespoons tomato paste, divided

2 tablespoons chopped fresh parsley

4 bell peppers, preferably different colors, stemmed, seeded, top portions set aside (as lids)

WORTH THE WAIT Dolmeh Felfel makes a delicious and beautiful appetizer, especially if the bell peppers are different colors. The filling can be anything from just rice and vegetables to ground beef or chicken. This is my family's version of the traditional recipe, with a stuffing made of rice, onion, garlic, ground beef, and plenty of herbs and spices.

1. In a medium saucepan, combine the rice, 1½ to 2 cups of water, a pinch of salt, and 1 tablespoon of vegetable oil. Bring the mixture to a boil over high heat, then let it cook uncovered until the rice is tender and the water has almost completely evaporated, about 20 minutes.

2. While the rice is cooking, in a large skillet, heat the remaining 2 tablespoons of vegetable oil over medium heat. Add the onion and sauté for about 10 minutes or until it is golden brown. Add the minced garlic and cook for another minute. Add in the ground beef, remaining ½ teaspoon of salt, cayenne, and turmeric. Cook, stirring frequently, until most of the water has evaporated and the ground beef is cooked completely, about 5 minutes. Add 1 tablespoon of tomato paste and the chopped parsley. Cook for another minute, then remove the skillet from the heat.

3. In a large bowl, mix together the ground beef mixture and the cooked rice. Fill the bell peppers with the rice and beef filling and top each one with its stem-end "lid."

4. In a large pot, mix together the remaining 1 tablespoon of tomato paste and 1 cup of water. Place the stuffed peppers in the pot, cover, and cook for 30 to 40 minutes or until the peppers are easily pierced with a knife.

5. Serve warm.

COOKING TIP Sometimes I like to use a combination of ground beef and lamb in this recipe for better taste and texture. You can also leave out the meat and use only rice and some vegetables, such as carrots and peas, for a vegan version of Dolmeh Felfel.

3 KOOKOOS & EGG DISHES

ZUCCHINI FRITTATA

کوکو کدو — KOOKOO KADOO

Serves 4
Prep: 15 minutes
Cook: 20 minutes

3 large zucchini

1 large yellow onion

3 garlic cloves, minced

2 tablespoons chopped
fresh dill

3 large eggs

2 tablespoons
all-purpose flour

½ teaspoon ground turmeric

1 teaspoon salt

½ teaspoon freshly ground
black pepper

3 to 4 tablespoons
vegetable oil

VEGETARIAN Kookoo Kadoo is made throughout Iran when zucchini are in season. The flavor gets a kick from the addition of garlic and dill, and it makes the perfect appetizer or lunch when served with fresh bread and some thick yogurt. While frittatas are usually made in large skillets or pans in the West, in Iran they are more like smaller egg pancakes, as in this recipe.

1. Grate the zucchini and onion. Squeeze them well in a clean kitchen towel or place them in a fine-mesh colander and press them with the back of a wooden spoon to extract as much liquid as possible. Discard the excess water.

2. In a large bowl, mix together the zucchini and onion, garlic, dill, eggs, flour, turmeric, salt, and pepper until well combined.

3. Heat the oil in a nonstick skillet over medium heat. Using a large spoon, drop a spoonful of the kookoo mixture into the hot oil. Fry for about 3 minutes, until the bottom is golden brown, then flip the kookoo and fry it on the other side for 3 minutes more. Transfer the cooked kookoo to a paper towel–lined plate and repeat the cooking process until all the batter is used up.

4. Serve hot.

COOKING TIP Instead of frying, you can bake Kookoo Kadoo in an 8-by-8-inch pan in a 350°F oven for 40 minutes. Just spray the pan with nonstick cooking spray before you add the batter.

POTATO FRITTATA

کوکو سیب زمینی KOOKOO SIBZAMINI

Serves 4
Prep: 30 minutes
Cook: 40 minutes

4 medium white potatoes

4 large eggs

2 tablespoons
all-purpose flour

1 teaspoon salt

½ teaspoon freshly ground
black pepper

1 teaspoon bloomed
saffron (see page 21)

1 tablespoon dried mint

½ teaspoon ground turmeric

¼ cup vegetable oil

Sliced tomatoes and pickles
for serving (optional)

VEGETARIAN Kookoo Sibzamini is one of the easiest
kookoos in the Persian kitchen. It requires just a hand-
ful of ingredients and is very economical. Because
potatoes are *sardi* (cool or cooling), my maman
always adds some dried mint to balance the dish.

1. Bring a large pot of water to a boil over medium heat and
boil the potatoes until they are fork tender, about 30 minutes.
(Alternatively, you can cook the potatoes in the microwave
until tender.) Drain the pot and transfer the potatoes to a plate
to cool. When they are cool enough to handle, peel the potatoes
and then mash them using a potato masher or purée them in
a food processor.

2. In a large bowl, mix together the mashed potatoes, eggs,
flour, salt, pepper, bloomed saffron, dried mint, and turmeric.
Mix well using a wooden spoon or a small spatula.

3. Using your hands, form the mixture into small patties. Wet
your hands before you form each potato patty to keep the batter
from sticking.

4. Heat the vegetable oil in a medium nonstick skillet over
medium heat. When the oil begins to shimmer, slide a few of the
potato patties into the skillet. Fry the patties for 3 to 4 minutes
on each side, then transfer them to a paper towel–lined plate
to drain. Repeat with the remaining patties.

5. Serve warm with fresh tomatoes and pickles.

MAKE IT EASIER You can bake these patties on a large,
parchment-lined baking sheet in a 375°F oven for 40 minutes.
Flip them halfway through.

EGGPLANT FRITTATA

کوکو بادمجان KOOKOO BADEMJAAN

Serves 4
Prep: 10 minutes
Cook: 30 minutes

3 medium eggplants

1 onion

3 garlic cloves, minced

4 large eggs

3 tablespoons
chopped walnuts

½ teaspoon salt

½ teaspoon freshly ground
black pepper

½ teaspoon ground turmeric

2 tablespoons vegetable oil

VEGETARIAN Kookoo Bademjaan is one of my favorite dishes. It's easy to make and very tasty, and it's a great vegetarian option—full of nutrient-dense eggplant, onion, garlic, walnuts, and spices. Walnut is a *garmi* (heating) food, so it balances the eggplant, which is *sardi* (cooling).

1. Peel and grate the eggplants and onion. Squeeze them well in a clean kitchen towel or place them in a fine-mesh colander and press them with the back of a wooden spoon, extracting as much liquid as possible. Discard the excess water.

2. In a large bowl, mix together the eggplant and onion, minced garlic, eggs, walnuts, salt, pepper, and turmeric until well combined.

3. Heat the vegetable oil in a medium nonstick skillet over medium heat. Pour all the kookoo batter into the pan. Cook for 15 minutes, until the bottom is golden brown, then flip the kookoo and cook the other side for another 15 minutes until it is set and golden brown on both sides.

WHY IT WORKS **Squeezing the grated eggplant releases the bitter juice. Squeezing the grated onion helps keep the kookoo from being too wet and falling apart.**

LENTIL FRITTATA

كوكو عدس KOOKOO ADAS

Serves 4
Prep: 30 minutes
Cook: 30 minutes

1 cup dried lentils, rinsed

2 white potatoes, peeled and chopped into small pieces

2 large eggs

1 teaspoon salt

½ teaspoon freshly ground black pepper

2 tablespoons chopped fresh parsley

2 tablespoons breadcrumbs

3 to 4 tablespoons vegetable oil

VEGETARIAN Kookoo Adas is a great way to have a nutritious meal without a lot of effort. They taste like beef patties but without the beef, with a texture similar to veggie burgers.

1. Place the lentils and potatoes in a large pot and cover them with water. Place the pot over high heat, bring the water to a boil, and cook uncovered for about 20 to 30 minutes or until the lentils and potatoes are tender. Drain well, return the lentils and potatoes to the pot, and mash them with a potato masher, or transfer them to a food processor and purée until smooth.

2. In a large bowl, mix together the mashed lentils and potatoes, eggs, salt, pepper, parsley, and breadcrumbs. Make sure everything is well incorporated.

3. Using your hands, form the mixture into small patties. Wet your hands before you form each patty to keep the batter from sticking.

4. Heat the vegetable oil in a medium skillet over medium heat. When the oil begins to shimmer, slide a few of the patties into the skillet. Fry the patties for 3 to 4 minutes on each side, then transfer them to a paper towel–lined plate to drain. Repeat with the remaining patties.

MAKE IT EASIER You can use canned cooked lentils (not lentil soup) for this recipe; just drain and rinse them well before mashing. You can also pour all the kookoo batter into the pan at once, then cook each side for 15 minutes or until the frittata is browned and set.

GREEN BEAN FRITTATA

کوکو لوبیا سبز KOOKOO LOOBIA SABZ

Serves 4
Prep: 20 minutes
Cook: 50 minutes

1 pound fresh green beans, trimmed and finely chopped

2 carrots, peeled and finely chopped

6 tablespoons vegetable oil, divided

2 medium white potatoes, peeled and cut into ½-inch cubes

1 red onion, chopped

½ pound lean ground beef

1 teaspoon salt

1 teaspoon freshly ground black pepper

½ teaspoon ground turmeric

5 large eggs

3 tablespoons barberries, rinsed and dried

WORTH THE WAIT Kookoo Loobia Sabz, originally from northwestern Iran, is full of delicious vegetables and ground beef, and can be eaten as a meal all on its own; just serve it with some Cucumber & Tomato Salad (page 40) or a bowl of plain Greek yogurt.

1. Using a double boiler, steam the green beans and carrots until tender, 7 to 9 minutes.

2. While the green beans and carrots are cooking, heat 2 tablespoons of vegetable oil in a large nonstick skillet over medium-high heat and sauté the potatoes until they are golden brown and tender, 10 to 15 minutes. Transfer to a bowl and set aside.

3. In the same skillet, heat 1 tablespoon of vegetable oil over medium-high heat and sauté the onion until it is translucent. Add the ground beef, salt, pepper, and turmeric. Cook, stirring frequently, until the ground beef is completely browned, about 5 minutes.

4. Squeeze the green beans and carrots in a clean kitchen towel or place them in a fine-mesh colander and press them with the back of a wooden spoon to extract as much liquid as possible. Discard the excess water.

5. In a large bowl, whisk the eggs, then add the vegetables and the beef mixture. Mix everything until well incorporated. Add the barberries and stir a little until just mixed.

6. Heat the remaining 3 tablespoons of vegetable oil in a clean, medium nonstick skillet over medium heat. Pour the kookoo batter into the pan all at once. Wrap the lid in a towel and cover the pan.

7. Cook for 15 minutes. Take the lid off, flip the kookoo, and cover the skillet with the towel-wrapped lid. Cook for another 10 minutes or until the frittata is set and browned on both sides.

8. Cut into wedges and serve hot.

COOKING TIP You can bake this kookoo in the oven. Coat an oven-safe dish with nonstick cooking spray, pour the batter in the dish, and cover it loosely with aluminum foil. Bake at 400°F for 30 minutes or until the frittata is set and browned at the edges.

HERB FRITTATA

کوکو سبزی KOOKOO SABZI

Serves 4
Prep: 15 minutes
Cook: 30 minutes

½ cup finely chopped
fresh parsley

½ cup finely chopped
fresh cilantro

½ cup finely chopped
fresh chives

1 cup finely chopped
fresh dill

4 large eggs

2 tablespoons
all-purpose flour

2 tablespoons
chopped walnuts

1 tablespoon barberries,
rinsed and dried

1 teaspoon salt

½ teaspoon ground turmeric

3 tablespoons vegetable oil

VEGETARIAN Kookoo Sabzi is served during Norooz celebrations—the Persian New Year—accompanied by Herbs & Rice (page 106). The barberries and walnuts are optional, but in my opinion, they take this traditional, herbaceous dish to a whole new level.

1. In a large bowl, mix together the parsley, cilantro, chives, dill, eggs, flour, walnuts, barberries, salt, and turmeric. Mix thoroughly until everything is fully incorporated.

2. Heat the vegetable oil in a medium nonstick skillet over medium heat, and pour in the kookoo batter all at once. Wrap the lid in a towel and cover the pan.

3. Cook for 15 minutes. Take the lid off, flip the kookoo, then cover the skillet with the towel-wrapped lid. Cook for another 15 minutes or until the frittata is set and browned on both sides.

4. Cut into wedges and serve hot.

COOKING TIP Wrapping the lid in a towel will help absorb the steam from the kookoo and keep it from leaking back into the batter. This will help the dish brown evenly.

SPINACH & EGGS

 نرگسی NARGESI

Serves 5
Prep: 10 minutes
Cook: 20 minutes

2 tablespoons olive oil

1 medium yellow onion, thinly sliced

1 (6-ounce) bag baby spinach, chopped

1 teaspoon ground turmeric

1 teaspoon bloomed saffron (see page 21)

½ teaspoon salt

1 teaspoon freshly ground black pepper

5 large eggs

VEGETARIAN, QUICK & EASY Nargesi is mostly a breakfast item in Iran, made with eggs, spinach, and warming spices, but if you serve it with bread, this nutritious dish can be a satisfying lunch or light dinner. For some extra tanginess, add a few chopped leeks (white parts only) to the pan along with the onion.

1. Heat the olive oil in a large nonstick skillet over medium heat and sauté the onion for 5 to 7 minutes or until it is soft and just beginning to turn golden in color. Add the spinach to the skillet and sauté until it is wilted and cooked through, 2 to 3 minutes, then add the turmeric, bloomed saffron, salt, and pepper and sauté until fragrant, about 1 minute.

2. Crack the eggs into the skillet and cover it with a lid. Cook until the eggs are cooked through but the yolks are still soft, 7 to 8 minutes.

3. Serve the Nargesi hot, right out of the skillet.

COOKING TIP You can cook the eggs a bit more, until the yolks are firm. You can also stir the eggs right after you break them, if you prefer a dish that's more like an omelet.

My Memories

We used to go on a road trip to the north of Iran at least twice a year. We packed everything, including some small pots and pans for our picnic, then hit the road to beautiful Chaloos, stopping first at a local shop that had the best yogurt and Doogh (yogurt drink) and also sold local eggs, fresh bread, and other goodies. When we got hungry for breakfast, we'd pull over, set up our little portable charcoal grill on the side of the road, and cook up an omelet using the eggs and whatever fresh vegetables we had packed up from the garden.

The smell of freshly charred eggplant and tomatoes mixed with local fresh eggs and tons of garlic is one I will never forget.

The road on both sides was green and full of tall trees, with paths cut through the forest for camping and cooking. Before we made it to our first campsite, we stopped at another local grocery store to get fresh tomatoes and eggplants that my dad and brother roasted over charcoal for Mirza Ghasemi (page 55). Then it was always my brother's wife who made the lunch, as she prepared it better than anyone else in our family.

The smell of freshly charred eggplant and tomatoes mixed with local fresh eggs and tons of garlic is one I will never forget. All the garlic in the dish would make us very sleepy, so we all went into our tents to take a good nap. After that, we had some tea and got on the road again toward our final destination. By evening we arrived, left our bags at the place we were staying, and went to one of the local restaurants to have a homey, delicious dinner. Whenever I think of those days, a big smile comes to my face and I just can't help thinking how magical they were.

SMOKY EGGPLANT & EGGS

میرزا قاسمی MIRZA GHASEMI

Serves 4
Prep: 10 minutes
Cook: 40 minutes

4 medium eggplants

6 large tomatoes

Nonstick cooking spray

2 tablespoons olive oil

6 garlic cloves, minced

1 teaspoon salt

½ teaspoon freshly ground black pepper

½ teaspoon ground turmeric

1 tablespoon tomato paste (optional)

4 large eggs

VEGETARIAN Mirza Ghasemi is a unique egg-based dish from the north of Iran, featuring charred eggplant and tomatoes. The smoky aroma from the eggplant gives this dish its depth and rich flavor. It can be a full meal on its own if it's served with some rice, preferably Kateh (page 22). Insider tip: Have something sweet for dessert after eating Mirza Ghasemi, as it contains a lot of garlic.

1. Preheat a charcoal grill to medium-high. Pierce the eggplants and tomatoes a few times using a fork. Grill them until tender and charred on all sides, about 30 minutes total. Remove the vegetables from the grill and set them aside to cool. When they are cool enough to handle, carefully remove the stems and peel off the skins. If you don't have a charcoal grill, preheat the oven to 400°F. Line a baking sheet with aluminum foil and then coat it with nonstick cooking spray. Place the pierced eggplants and tomatoes on the prepared baking sheet, roast for 25 to 35 minutes or until the vegetables are completely soft, then turn the oven to broil. Broil the vegetables for 5 minutes so the skin chars a bit, flipping them halfway through, then remove the baking sheet from the oven, let the vegetables cool completely, and carefully peel off the skins.

2. Place the cooked and peeled eggplants and tomatoes in separate bowls and mash them with a potato masher.

3. Heat the olive oil in a large nonstick skillet over medium heat and sauté the garlic for 1 minute. Add the mashed tomatoes, let them cook for 5 minutes, then add the mashed eggplant, salt, pepper, and turmeric.

4. Cook until all the water from the tomatoes evaporates. If the color of the dish is not as red as you would like, stir in the tomato paste.

5. Break the eggs in the pan, and stir until they are fully incorporated. Cook for another 5 minutes or until the eggs have set.

6. Serve warm with bread or rice.

MAKE IT EASIER Swap out the fresh eggplant for 64 ounces of canned fire-roasted eggplant purée, which is available in Asian and Middle Eastern stores.

EGGS & TOMATOES

OMLET ‏املت‏

Serves 4
Prep: 10 minutes
Cook: 15 minutes

6 large tomatoes

3 tablespoons vegetable oil

½ tablespoon tomato paste

1 teaspoon salt

4 large eggs

VEGETARIAN, QUICK & EASY Omlet is a very common "easy" food in Iran. It can be served for breakfast, lunch, or dinner, and you can find eggs and tomatoes in almost everyone's kitchen. Some families add chopped parsley or diced green bell peppers for more flavor, and we always served ours with fresh herbs and bread on the side.

1. In a large bowl, grate the tomatoes and discard any large pieces of the skin. (This is definitely easier in a food processor, if you have one.)

2. In a large nonstick skillet, heat the vegetable oil over medium heat. Add the grated tomatoes and cook until the juice has evaporated and the tomatoes have thickened, about 10 minutes. Add the tomato paste and salt. Stir until combined.

3. Crack the eggs into the skillet and immediately stir everything together. Keep stirring until the eggs are fully cooked, about 3 to 4 minutes.

4. Serve hot.

MAKE IT EASIER **You can use canned whole peeled tomatoes instead of fresh tomatoes.**

POTATOES & EGGS

يرالما يومورتا YERALMA YUMURTA

Serves 4
Prep: 5 minutes
Cook: 30 minutes

4 medium white potatoes

4 large eggs

2 tablespoons unsalted butter, melted (optional)

1½ teaspoons salt

1 teaspoon freshly ground black pepper

Fresh bread, for serving (preferably lavash or flour tortillas)

1 teaspoon dried mint (optional)

VEGETARIAN Yeralma Yumurta is one of the most popular street foods from Tabriz, a city in the northwest of Iran where my baba is from, and where people speak Azeri. In Azeri, *yeralma* means potato and *yumurta* means egg. This dish is easy, delicious, filling, and very healthy, and we eat a lot of it.

1. Put the potatoes in a large pot and cover them with water. Place the pot over high heat, bring the water to a boil, and cook the potatoes uncovered for 30 minutes or until they are easily pierced with a knife. Drain well and set the potatoes aside to cool.

2. Meanwhile, place the eggs in a medium saucepan and cover them with water. Bring the water to a boil over high heat, then immediately turn off the heat and cover the pan. Let the eggs sit in the hot water for 10 minutes, then drain them and set them aside to cool. The eggs should be hard-boiled.

3. When the potatoes and eggs are cool enough to handle, peel them and mash them together in a large bowl using a potato masher. Alternatively, you can transfer the peeled potatoes and eggs to a food processor and purée until smooth.

4. Add the melted butter (if using) to the bowl, along with the salt and pepper. Mix well.

5. Serve the Yeralma Yumurta on the bread, topped with dried mint (if using).

BEYOND THE BASICS Sometimes I add crumbled feta cheese and omit the salt in this recipe. It's a delicious variation, if you like cheese with potatoes.

OLIVIER SALAD

سالاد الویه SALAD OLIVIEH

Serves 4
Prep: 10 minutes,
plus 1 hour for chilling
Cook: 1 hour

4 potatoes

½ boneless chicken breast

4 eggs

1 cup green peas

1 carrot, diced

2 large pickled
cucumbers, diced

1 cup mayonnaise

1 teaspoon salt

WORTH THE WAIT Salad Olvieh is actually a Russian dish that has found its way into the cuisines of many nearby countries, including Iran. The specific recipe varies a bit from country to country, but the base of most of them is potatoes, eggs, carrots, peas, and pickled cucumbers. You can easily make this vegetarian by leaving out the chicken, and to make it healthier, use light mayonnaise or even Greek yogurt.

1. Put the potatoes in a large pot and cover them with water. Place the pot over high heat, bring the water to a boil, and cook the potatoes uncovered for 30 minutes or until they are easily pierced with a knife. Drain well and set the potatoes aside to cool.

2. Meanwhile, place the chicken in a medium saucepan and cover it with water. Place the pan over high heat and bring the water to a boil. Cook the chicken uncovered for 15 to 20 minutes or until it registers 165°F on an instant-read thermometer. Drain well and set the chicken aside to cool.

3. Place the eggs in another medium saucepan and cover them with water. Bring the water to a boil over high heat, then immediately turn off the heat and cover the pan. Let the eggs sit in the hot water for 10 minutes, then drain them and set them aside to cool. The eggs should be hard-boiled.

4. In a steamer pot or a heatproof colander set over a pot of boiling water, steam the peas and carrots until tender, 8 to 10 minutes. Remove the pot from the heat and set it aside.

5. When the potatoes and eggs are cool enough to handle, peel them and place them in a large bowl. Shred the cooked chicken breast using two forks.

6. Mash the potatoes and eggs with a potato masher, then mix in the shredded chicken breast. Add the peas, carrots, and pickled cucumbers to the bowl and toss well, then mix in the mayonnaise and salt.

7. Cover the bowl and refrigerate the salad for at least 1 hour before serving.

MAKE IT EASIER Use frozen peas and carrots for this recipe, and just microwave them according to the instructions on the package, to save time.

4 SOUPS & ASH

COLD YOGURT SOUP

آبدوغ خیار ABDOOGH KHIAR

Serves 4
Prep: 15 minutes,
plus 5 to 7 minutes
for soaking

2 cups plain yogurt

5 cups cold water

1 teaspoon salt

2 teaspoons dried mint

2 Persian cucumbers or any
seedless cucumber, diced

4 tablespoons raisins

4 tablespoons
chopped walnuts

1 cup chopped fresh herbs
(mint, parsley, dill, and basil)

2 teaspoons powdered
Persian rose petals (optional)

Ice cubes

Dry thin bread, for serving

VEGETARIAN, QUICK & EASY Abdoogh Khiar is a great dish for hot summer days because it's light, cold, and full of ingredients that balance body temperature in the heat. In my family we always have this soup at least once a week on hot days, and we serve it with very dry thin bread. You can find powdered dried rose petals in Middle Eastern supermarkets. To grind them yourself, just pulse some dried petals in a coffee grinder a few times.

1. Mix the yogurt, water, salt, and dried mint in a blender or food processor and purée until the mixture is smooth and uniform in color.

2. Divide the cucumbers, raisins, walnuts, and herbs among four bowls.

3. Pour one quarter of the yogurt mixture into each bowl.

4. Top with powdered dried Persian rose petals (if using), and add a few ice cubes to each bowl.

5. Tear the dry thin bread into small pieces and add some to each bowl. Let the bread pieces soak for 5 to 7 minutes before serving.

6. Serve cold.

INGREDIENT TIP **You can make your own dry bread. Cut flatbread or flour tortillas into small pieces and bake them in a 400°F oven for 15 minutes, until crispy and dry.**

GREEN LENTIL SOUP

عدسی ADASI

Serves 4
Prep: 10 minutes,
plus overnight to soak
the lentils
Cook: 45 minutes

2 cups dried green lentils,
soaked in water overnight

2 tablespoons olive oil

1 medium yellow onion,
finely chopped

1 medium white potato,
peeled and cut into
small cubes

4 cups water or
vegetable stock

1 teaspoon salt

½ teaspoon cayenne pepper

VEGAN Adasi is a soothing, hearty soup that's easy to make and is common in Iranian households. The consistency and ingredients vary from family to family, so feel free to experiment until you get the combination that is just to your taste. It can be served for breakfast, brunch, or a light dinner. Soaking the lentils in water will not only help them cook faster, but will also make them easier to digest.

1. Drain the lentils and rinse them well under running water.

2. Heat the olive oil in a large pot over medium heat and sauté the onion until it is golden brown, about 10 minutes. Add the lentils and sauté for 5 minutes, then add the chopped potato and water or stock.

3. Bring the soup to a boil, then reduce the heat to low and simmer for 20 to 30 minutes, uncovered, until the lentils and potatoes are tender. Check every 10 minutes and add ½ cup more water if needed.

4. When the soup is done, stir in the salt and cayenne.

5. Serve warm with some bread.

MAKE IT EASIER You can put all the ingredients in a slow cooker and cook it on low for 7 to 8 hours.

POTATO & EGG SOUP

اشکنه سیب زمینی ESHKENEH SIBZAMINI

Serves 4
Prep: 15 minutes
Cook: 1 hour, 10 minutes

2 tablespoons vegetable oil

1 large yellow onion,
finely chopped

2 large white potatoes,
cut into cubes

1 tablespoon all-purpose flour

1 teaspoon ground turmeric

1 tablespoon dried
fenugreek leaves

3 cups water

3 large eggs

½ teaspoon salt

½ teaspoon freshly ground
black pepper

WHY IT WORKS Adding
some hot soup to the eggs
before pouring the eggs
into the soup brings them
up to almost the same
temperature. This helps
the eggs blend better
with the soup.

VEGETARIAN, WORTH THE WAIT Eshkeneh is an old peasant-food soup that is famous in northeastern Iran. It might not seem all that exciting, with an ingredient list bolstered by just onion, potatoes, and eggs, but the magic here is in the seasonings—namely the dried fenugreek leaves. Fenugreek has been found at cooking sites dating back to 4,000 BCE. Both the leaves and the seeds have a sweet, nutty, vegetable flavor. If you can find fresh fenugreek leaves, feel free to chop up a half cup and use them instead of the dried.

1. Heat the vegetable oil in a large pot over medium heat. When the oil begins to shimmer, add the onion and sauté until it's golden brown, about 10 minutes. Add the potatoes and flour and cook, stirring constantly, for 6 to 8 minutes, until the potatoes are golden on all sides. Add the turmeric and fenugreek and sauté until the spices become fragrant, 1 to 2 minutes.

2. Add the water to the pot and bring the soup to a boil. Let the soup cook uncovered for 25 to 30 minutes.

3. Crack the eggs into a small bowl and beat them with a fork. Add 3 tablespoons of boiling soup to the eggs and stir vigorously, then stir the egg mixture into the boiling soup.

4. Cook the soup for another 10 to 15 minutes, until the eggs are cooked and the soup is thick. Add the salt and pepper and stir well to incorporate.

5. Serve hot.

VERMICELLI SOUP

سوپ رشته SOOPE RESHTEH

Serves 4
Prep: 10 minutes
Cook: 1 hour

1 tablespoon vegetable oil

1 medium yellow onion, finely chopped

½ boneless, skinless chicken breast, cut into small pieces

1 carrot, peeled and cut into small pieces

1 large white potato, cut into cubes

1 cup green peas (fresh or frozen)

5 to 6 cups water

2 tablespoons tomato paste

½ teaspoon salt

3 ounces dried vermicelli

¼ cup chopped fresh parsley

Fresh lemon wedges, for serving

WORTH THE WAIT If you have a cold or just feel like you need something easy and tasty, this soup is for you. Because Soope Reshteh contains a lot of vegetables, it's very nutritious and makes a perfect full meal. We always add some freshly squeezed lemon juice to the soup just before serving, to give it a bit of tanginess.

1. Heat the vegetable oil in a large pot over medium heat. When the oil begins to shimmer, add the onion and sauté until it's translucent, about 5 minutes. Add the chicken breast and sauté until the pieces are no longer pink, 2 or 3 minutes. Add the carrot, potato, and green peas, then pour in the water. Bring the soup to a boil, then reduce the heat to low and simmer uncovered for 30 minutes or until the carrot and potato are tender.

2. Add the tomato paste and salt to the pot and stir until they are fully incorporated. Add the vermicelli and cook for 10 minutes more, until the noodles are tender and the soup thickens a bit.

3. Add the chopped fresh parsley and cook for 5 minutes more.

4. Serve hot with lemon wedges.

MAKE IT EASIER If you have some cooked chicken, cut it into small pieces and add it at the end with the tomato paste and salt. You can also use canned green peas, adding them with the tomato paste and salt so they don't break down.

OATMEAL SOUP

سوپ جو SOOPE JO

Serves 4
Prep: 5 minutes
Cook: 45 minutes

2 tablespoons vegetable oil

1 medium yellow onion, finely chopped

1 large carrot, peeled and grated

1 cup old-fashioned rolled oats

½ cup diced boneless, skinless chicken breast

3 cups water

1 cup whole milk

1 tablespoon all-purpose flour

¼ cup chopped fresh parsley

1 teaspoon salt

1 teaspoon freshly ground black pepper

Fresh lemon wedges, for serving

Old-fashioned rolled oats are a breakfast food in the United States, but they also make a wonderful, savory Persian soup—perfect for serving as a first course for winter dinner parties. The milk gives this chicken-and-vegetable soup a mild and smooth taste and texture, which is offset by a hearty dose of black pepper and a squeeze of lemon juice at the end. If it's too spicy for your taste, just reduce the amount of black pepper.

1. Heat the vegetable oil in a large pot over medium heat. When the oil begins to shimmer, add the onion and sauté until it's translucent, about 5 minutes. Add the carrot and stir for 2 to 3 minutes, then add the oats and chicken and sauté until the chicken pieces are no longer pink, 2 to 3 minutes.

2. Pour in the water and bring it to a boil, then reduce the heat to low and let the soup simmer for 20 to 25 minutes, until the chicken is cooked through. Add more water if needed, but not too much. The soup is supposed to be somewhat thick.

3. In a separate bowl, use a spoon to mix together the milk and flour. Pour 4 to 5 tablespoons of the hot soup into the milk mixture, stir well, then pour the milk mixture very slowly into the soup, stirring constantly. Let the soup simmer for another 10 minutes, then stir in the parsley, salt, and pepper.

4. Serve hot with fresh lemon wedges.

SUBSTITUTION TIP **Leave out the chicken for a vegetarian soup. You can add some chopped mushrooms instead, if you like.**

LAMB LOIN SOUP

سوپ ماهیچه SOOPE MAHICHEH

Serves 4
Prep: 10 minutes,
plus overnight to
soak the lentils
Cook: 1 hour

1 medium yellow onion,
finely chopped

3 garlic cloves, minced

1 pound lamb loin, cut into
½-inch cubes

¼ teaspoon ground turmeric

5 cups water

2 carrots, peeled and cut
into small pieces

1 small white potato, cut
into small pieces

½ cup dried lentils, soaked in
water overnight and drained

½ cup long-grain white rice,
such as basmati, rinsed
and drained

1 teaspoon salt

½ teaspoon freshly ground
black pepper

½ cup chopped fresh parsley

Fresh lemon wedges,
for serving

WORTH THE WAIT I have a lot of happy memories associated with this soup, as my late grandmother always used to make it. It's just what you need on cold winter days. It's thick, very hearty, and filling, and very easy to make. Most of the ingredients used are items that are always in your kitchen. If lamb loin is not something that you keep in your freezer, it can easily be replaced by chicken. If you're using chicken breast pieces, cut the cooking time in half in step 2 (before you add the vegetables).

1. In a large pot, combine the onion, garlic, lamb loin, turmeric, and water. Bring the liquid to a boil over high heat, then reduce the heat to low and simmer uncovered for 25 minutes. At this point, the lamb pieces should be brown on the outside but still red on the inside.

2. Add the carrots, potato, lentils, and rice to the pot, stir well, and simmer for another 25 minutes or until everything is tender and fully cooked. Stir in the salt and pepper, then taste the broth and add more salt if needed. Stir in the parsley and cook for 5 more minutes.

3. Serve hot with fresh lemon wedges.

COOKING TIP **If you would like an even thicker soup, mix 1 tablespoon all-purpose flour with ⅓ cup water and add it to the soup with the rice and lentils.**

My Memories

Iranians have a very special way of eating Ab-Goosht. There are two parts to the dish: *terid* and *goosht koobideh*. *Terid* is the gravy or juice that the meat and other ingredients have cooked in. We pour the gravy into a bowl and add small pieces of dry, crispy bread—preferably lavash. (To make your own dry, crispy bread, see the recipe for Cold Yogurt Soup on page 64.) We eat the gravy with a spoon, like a soup with crackers in it.

> *For my family, Ab-Goosht is a meal we love eating together, and we spend a long time around the table enjoying it.*

Next comes the *goosht koobideh*, the meat and other ingredients that were cooked in the gravy. The traditional way to prepare this is to grab a masher (a potato masher is perfect) and mash everything until it is blended together in a sticky mixture. You can eat goosht koobideh on its own or with bread. On the side, fresh herbs, red onions, and pickled vegetables are a must.

For my family, Ab-Goosht is a meal we love eating together, and we spend a long time around the table enjoying it. The lamb my maman uses for Ab-Goosht is always the freshest. My dad did the mashing part and my mom added the final spices. Then they served the whole thing with fresh herbs and red onion.

LAMB & CHICKPEA STEW

آبگوشت AB-GOOSHT

Serves 4
Prep: 10 minutes,
plus overnight to soak
the beans
Cook: 1 hour, 20 minutes

1 cup dried chickpeas, soaked
in water overnight

1 cup dried white beans,
soaked in water overnight

1 pound lamb loin, cut
into 2-inch cubes

2 medium yellow onions,
finely chopped

6 cups water

3 medium white potatoes,
peeled and halved

3 tablespoons tomato paste

2 teaspoons salt

1 teaspoon freshly ground
black pepper

1 teaspoon ground cinnamon

Dry crispy thin bread,
preferably lavash, for serving

Mixed chopped fresh herbs,
for serving

Red onion slices, for serving

Pickled vegetables,
for serving

WORTH THE WAIT Ab-Goosht is a popular and much loved dish in Iran, made of lamb and beans simmered in a mixture of water and tomato paste. The recipe couldn't be easier to follow (basically, you just dump everything in the pot), and it works well in a slow cooker, too. Unlike an American-style stew, once everything is cooked, the meat and beans are taken out of the gravy, mashed, and served on the side, and the gravy is served in a bowl with bread. This dish is best with some fresh herbs such as basil, parsley, and chives—and of course, some pickled vegetables and raw red onion.

1. Drain the chickpeas and white beans. Put them in a large pot, then add the lamb, onions, and water. Place the pot over medium-high heat and bring the water to a boil, then reduce the heat to medium, cover the pot, and let the stew cook for 40 to 50 minutes or until the beans are tender and the lamb is cooked through.

2. When the lamb and beans are cooked and tender, add the potatoes and tomato paste to the pot and stir well to dissolve the tomato paste. Cover the pot and cook for another 30 minutes, until the potatoes are tender. Stir in the salt and pepper.

3. Using a large slotted spoon, remove the lamb, beans, and potatoes from the pot and transfer them to a large bowl. Add the cinnamon and mash the mixture using a potato masher.

4. Pour the gravy into four individual serving bowls, add small pieces of dried bread to each bowl, and let them sit for a few minutes or until the bread softens a bit.

5. Arrange the meat and beans on a large platter and place the herbs, red onion slices, and pickled vegetables on a separate plate. Put a bowl of gravy and bread at each place setting, along with a small plate, and let everyone help themselves to the meat and beans and accoutrements.

MAKE IT EASIER Combine the chickpeas, white beans, lamb, chopped onion, water, potatoes, tomato paste, salt, and pepper in a slow cooker and cook on low for 8 hours. Then proceed from step 3. Or, use canned beans and chickpeas (drained and rinsed) to reduce the cooking time. First, cook the lamb and onion in water for about 40 to 50 minutes. When the lamb is cooked through, add the potatoes and tomato paste. When the potatoes are tender, add the canned beans. Then proceed from step 3.

TOMATO ASH

آش گوجه فرنگی ASH-E-GOJEH FARANGI

Serves 4
Prep: 10 minutes,
plus overnight to soak
the beans
Cook: 45 minutes

2 tablespoons vegetable oil

1 large yellow onion,
finely chopped

1 teaspoon ground turmeric

1 cup dried split chickpeas,
soaked in water overnight

1 cup long-grain white rice,
such as basmati, soaked in
water overnight

4 to 5 cups water

5 large tomatoes, peeled
and crushed

2 tablespoons tomato paste
(optional)

1 teaspoon salt

1½ teaspoons cayenne pepper
(or to taste)

½ cup chopped fresh spinach

¼ cup chopped fresh cilantro

¼ cup chopped fresh parsley

½ cup Persian verjuice

VEGAN, WORTH THE WAIT Ash-e-Gojeh Farangi is spicy and sour because it contains Persian verjuice (*abghoreh*), which is made from the tart juice of unripe grapes. The recipe also contains split chickpeas—not the same as the whole round ones. Split chickpeas are widely available in Indian grocery stores, where they are called chana dal.

1. Heat the vegetable oil in a large pot over medium heat. Sauté the onion until golden brown, about 10 minutes, then add the turmeric and cook for another 2 minutes.

2. Drain the split chickpeas and rice and add them to the pot with the onion. Stir well. Pour in the water, bring the ash to a boil, then reduce the heat to low and simmer until the split chickpeas and rice are tender, about 15 minutes. Check the ash after 10 minutes and add more water if needed. This ash should be thick, though, so you won't need much more water.

3. When the split chickpeas and rice are cooked, add the tomatoes to the pot. If the ash is not as red as you would like, add the tomato paste and stir well until it is completely dissolved. Stir in the salt and cayenne, let the ash simmer for 5 more minutes, then add the spinach, cilantro, and parsley. Stir in the Persian verjuice and cook for 10 minutes more or until the greens have wilted and everything is heated through.

4. Serve hot.

INGREDIENT TIP You can find Persian verjuice in Middle Eastern and Mediterranean supermarkets. You can also use freshly squeezed lemon juice instead of the Persian verjuice— just add it to the ash at the very end, right before serving.

YOGURT SOUP

آش دوغ ASH-E-DOOGH

Serves 6
Prep: 15 minutes,
plus overnight to soak
the beans
Cook: 1 hour, 35 minutes

FOR THE MEATBALLS

8 ounces lean ground beef

1 medium yellow onion,
grated and squeezed in
a clean kitchen towel

½ teaspoon salt

1 teaspoon vegetable oil

FOR THE YOGURT MIXTURE

3 cups plain yogurt

5 cups water

1 teaspoon salt

1 large egg

WORTH THE WAIT Ash-e-Doogh is one of the traditional dishes of the Azeri region in Iran. Because it has chickpeas and meatballs, this ash can be a full meal on its own. You can also leave out the meatballs; in the area around Ardebil, a city in the northwestern region, Ash-e-Doogh is vegetarian. For an authentic touch, sauté some dried mint in hot vegetable oil and top the ash with it. And be sure to have something sweet after this ash, because all that yogurt is *sardi* (cooling), and you want to balance it with something *garmi* (heating).

TO MAKE THE MEATBALLS

1. In a large bowl, mix together the ground beef, onion, and salt until well combined.

2. Using your hands, form the mixture into ½-inch meatballs.

3. Heat the vegetable oil in a large skillet over medium-high heat, and cook the meatballs until they are browned on all sides, 7 to 10 minutes. Remove the skillet from the heat and set it aside.

TO MAKE THE YOGURT MIXTURE

In a large bowl, whisk together the yogurt, water, salt, and egg until smooth. Cover and refrigerate.

FOR THE SOUP

1 cup dried chickpeas, soaked in water overnight

1 cup long-grain white rice, such as basmati, soaked in water and a pinch of salt for 1 hour

4 garlic cloves, minced

1 cup chopped fresh chives

1 cup chopped fresh parsley

1 cup chopped fresh dill (optional)

TO MAKE THE SOUP

1. Drain the chickpeas, place them in a medium pot, and cover them with water. Place the pot over high heat, bring the water to a boil, and cook uncovered until the chickpeas are tender, 30 to 40 minutes. Drain and set aside.

2. Drain the rice. In a large pot, mix the rice and garlic with the yogurt mixture. Place the pot over medium heat and cook for about 10 minutes or until the rice is cooked halfway (you will be able to break a rice grain in half using your fingers, but the center should still be hard). Then add the cooked chickpeas and cook for another 15 minutes, stirring occasionally.

3. Stir in the chives, parsley, and dill (if using), and add the cooked meatballs to the pot. Reduce the heat to low and simmer for 20 minutes, stirring constantly. Stirring is important to keep the rice from sticking to the bottom of the pot.

4. Serve hot.

MAKE IT EASIER You can use canned chickpeas (drained and rinsed) for this recipe; 1½ cans would be enough. Add the chickpeas when the rice is half cooked. You can also use leftover cooked white rice instead of raw rice. Skip the part in step 2 of the soup where you cook the rice halfway, and just pick up the recipe from where you add the chickpeas.

BARLEY ASH

آش جو ASH-E-JO

Serves 4
Prep: 10 minutes,
plus overnight to soak
the beans
Cook: 1 hour, 25 minutes

FOR THE SOUP

2 tablespoons vegetable oil

1 large onion, finely chopped

½ teaspoon ground turmeric

1 cup barley, soaked in
water overnight

½ cup dried chickpeas,
soaked in water overnight

½ cup dried pinto beans,
soaked in water overnight

½ cup dried lentils, soaked
in water overnight

4 to 5 cups water

½ cup chopped fresh parsley

½ cup chopped fresh cilantro

½ cup chopped fresh chives

1 cup chopped fresh spinach

1 teaspoon salt

FOR THE TOPPING

1 tablespoon vegetable oil

2 tablespoons dried mint

½ teaspoon ground turmeric

1 cup kashk (yogurt whey,
see page 39)

VEGETARIAN, WORTH THE WAIT Ash-e-Jo is made with barley, which is not a common grain in Persian cooking. The pinto beans and chickpeas make it very nutritious and satisfying. If you're using already cooked legumes, beans, or grains, add them after the barley is cooked.

TO MAKE THE SOUP

1. Heat the vegetable oil in a large pot over medium heat. Sauté the onion until golden brown, about 10 minutes, then stir in the turmeric.

2. Drain the barley, chickpeas, pinto beans, and lentils and add them to the pot with the onion. Pour in the water (the beans should be completely covered), bring it to a boil, then reduce the heat to low and simmer until the mixture is tender, about 1 hour. Check every 20 minutes and add more water if needed to keep the beans submerged.

3. When everything is fully cooked, add the parsley, cilantro, chives, and spinach. Cook for an additional 15 minutes, then stir in the salt.

TO MAKE THE TOPPING

1. Heat the vegetable oil in a small skillet over medium-high heat. Add the dried mint and sauté for 1 minute, then stir in the turmeric.

2. Serve the ash hot, topped with the sautéed mint and kashk.

MAKE IT EASIER If you didn't have a chance to soak the beans, chickpeas, and barley overnight, simply boil them in water for 30 minutes, then drain them and follow the recipe.

EGGPLANT ASH

آش بادمجان ASH-E-BADEMJAAN

Serves 4
Prep: 40 minutes,
plus overnight to soak
the beans
Cook: 1 hour, 15 minutes

FOR THE ASH

4 Chinese eggplants, peeled
and cut into 1-inch chunks

2 tablespoons vegetable oil

1 large yellow onion,
finely chopped

4 garlic cloves, minced

1 teaspoon ground turmeric

4¼ cups water, divided

1 cup dried chickpeas, soaked
in water overnight

¾ cup dried lentils, soaked
in water overnight

1 cup kashk (yogurt whey,
see page 39)

FOR THE TOPPING

1 tablespoon vegetable oil

2 tablespoons dried mint

½ teaspoon ground turmeric

VEGETARIAN, WORTH THE WAIT Eggplant is used frequently in Persian appetizers, main dishes, and even ash. If you don't have time to cook the chickpeas, feel free to use two 15-ounce cans instead. Just drain and rinse the canned chickpeas and add them when the lentils are completely cooked.

TO MAKE THE ASH

1. Sprinkle the eggplant chunks with salt and place them in a colander set over a large bowl to drain for about 30 minutes.

2. Heat the vegetable oil in a large pot over medium-high heat. Sauté the onion and garlic until golden, 6 to 8 minutes. Add the drained eggplant and turmeric to the pot, along with ¼ cup of water. Sauté until the eggplant is golden and soft, 5 to 7 minutes.

3. Drain the chickpeas and lentils and add them to the pot. Add the remaining 4 cups of water and stir well. Bring the liquid to a boil, then reduce the heat to low and simmer the ash until the chickpeas and lentils are tender, about 50 minutes.

4. Stir in the kashk and cook for another 10 minutes.

TO MAKE THE TOPPING

1. Heat the vegetable oil in a small skillet over medium heat. Sauté the dried mint and turmeric for 1 minute, then immediately remove the skillet from the heat.

2. Serve the hot ash topped with the sautéed dried mint.

COOKING TIP **Eggplants can soak up a lot of oil, and they can also release bitter juices when cooked. Salting and draining them in a colander helps improve their flavor and prevent them from getting too oily.**

SOUPS & ASH **77**

NOODLES & HERBS ASH

آش رشته ASH-E-RESHTEH

Serves 4
Prep: 20 minutes,
plus overnight to soak
the beans
Cook: 2 hours, 20 minutes

FOR THE ASH

2 tablespoons vegetable oil

2 medium yellow onions,
finely chopped

½ cup dried chickpeas,
soaked in water overnight

½ cup dried pinto beans,
soaked in water overnight

6 to 8 cups water

½ cup dried lentils, soaked
in water overnight

1 cup chopped fresh spinach

1 cup chopped fresh cilantro

1 cup chopped fresh parsley

8 ounces dried reshteh or
fettuccine noodles
(if using fettuccine,
add ½ teaspoon salt)

VEGETARIAN, WORTH THE WAIT Ash-e-Reshteh is one of the most famous dishes in Iran. *Reshteh* means noodles; the Persian noodles that are used in this dish are flat and similar to fettuccine. You can find reshteh in Persian or Mediterranean grocery stores. If you cannot find reshteh, you can use fettuccine instead and add ½ teaspoon salt. This dish is served with kashk, sautéed mint, fried garlic, and fried onions on top.

TO MAKE THE ASH

1. Heat the vegetable oil in a large pot over medium heat. When the oil begins to shimmer, add the onions and sauté until golden brown, about 10 minutes. Drain the chickpeas and pinto beans and add them to the pot with the onions. Stir well, then pour in the water. (The beans should be completely covered.)

2. Increase the heat to high, bring the liquid to a boil, then reduce the heat to medium, cover the pot, and cook for about 1 hour, until the chickpeas and beans are tender.

3. Drain the lentils and add them to the pot along with the spinach, cilantro, and parsley. Add more water if needed to keep the beans and lentils submerged. Cook for 30 to 40 minutes, until the lentils are tender.

4. Add the reshteh and cook for 20 minutes or until the noodles are soft and cooked through.

FOR THE TOPPING

2 tablespoons vegetable oil, divided

1 medium yellow onion, thinly sliced

3 garlic cloves, finely chopped

2 tablespoons dried mint

½ teaspoon ground turmeric

1 cup kashk (yogurt whey, see page 39)

TO MAKE THE TOPPING

1. Heat 1 tablespoon of vegetable oil in a small skillet over medium heat. When the oil begins to shimmer, add the onion and garlic and sauté until golden brown, about 10 minutes. Transfer the onion and garlic to a plate.

2. In the same skillet, heat the remaining 1 tablespoon of vegetable oil over medium heat, then add the dried mint and turmeric and sauté for 1 minute. Immediately remove the skillet from the heat.

3. Top each bowl of Ash-e-Reshteh with some caramelized onion and garlic, sautéed mint, and kashk.

MAKE IT EASIER You can use one 15-ounce can each of chickpeas and pinto beans. Just drain and rinse them, add them to the sautéed onion in step 1, add the water, and simmer for 20 to 30 minutes.

COOKING TIP If the ash is very watery, mix 1 tablespoon all-purpose flour with ½ cup water and add it to the pot after you add the reshteh.

POMEGRANATE ASH

آش انار ASH-E-ANAR

Serves 4
Prep: 20 minutes,
plus overnight to soak
the beans
Cook: 1 hour, 25 minutes

FOR THE MEATBALLS

8 ounces lean ground beef

1 small yellow onion, grated
and squeezed in a clean
kitchen towel

½ teaspoon salt

2 tablespoons vegetable oil

WORTH THE WAIT Ash-e-Anar is a delicious ash for autumn and winter. It has a sour taste because of the pomegranate juice and pomegranate molasses (also known as pomegranate syrup). Similar to many other Persian ash dishes, Ash-e-Anar is also topped with sautéed dried mint. The meatballs can be left out for a vegan version. If you decide to do that, add a can of kidney beans (drained and rinsed) to the ash with the salt in step 3 to give the dish some bulk.

TO MAKE THE MEATBALLS

1. In a large bowl, mix together the ground beef, grated onion, and salt.

2. Using your hands, form the meat mixture into ½-inch meatballs.

3. Heat the vegetable oil in a large skillet over medium heat. When the oil begins to shimmer, add the meatballs and cook until they are brown on all sides, 8 to 10 minutes. Remove the skillet from the heat and set aside.

FOR THE ASH

2 tablespoons vegetable oil

1 medium yellow onion, thinly sliced

1 cup dried split chickpeas, soaked in water overnight

1 cup long-grain white rice, such as basmati, soaked in water overnight

4 to 5 cups water

⅓ cup chopped fresh parsley

⅓ cup chopped fresh cilantro

½ cup chopped fresh spinach

2 cups pomegranate juice

2 tablespoons pomegranate molasses (optional)

1 teaspoon salt

FOR THE TOPPING

1 tablespoon vegetable oil

2 tablespoons dried mint

½ teaspoon ground turmeric

TO MAKE THE ASH

1. Heat the vegetable oil in a large pot over medium-high heat. When the oil begins to shimmer, add the onion and sauté until it's golden brown, about 10 minutes. Drain the split chickpeas and rice, add them to the onion, and give everything a nice stir. Then pour in the water, bring the liquid to a boil, and reduce the heat to medium. Cover the pot and let the ash simmer until the split chickpeas and rice are tender, about 45 minutes.

2. Add the parsley, cilantro, and spinach and cook for 10 minutes, stirring constantly, then add the pomegranate juice. Taste the broth; it should be sour and the pomegranate flavor should be noticeable. If it's not sour enough, stir in the pomegranate molasses.

3. Add the meatballs and salt to the pot and cook for 10 minutes, stirring constantly, until the meatballs are heated through.

TO MAKE THE TOPPING

1. Heat the vegetable oil in a small skillet over medium heat. Add the dried mint and turmeric and sauté for 1 minute, then immediately remove the skillet from the heat.

2. Serve the ash hot, topped with the sautéed dried mint and turmeric.

MAKE IT EASIER To save time, soak the rice in water for 1 hour and boil the split chickpeas for 20 minutes, then drain them both and follow the recipe.

5

STEWS & ACCOMPANYING RICE DISHES

PERSIAN HERB STEW

خورش قورمه سبزی KHORESH-E-GHORMEH SABZI

Serves 4
Prep: 20 minutes,
plus overnight to soak
the beans
Cook: 3 hours

4 cups finely chopped
fresh parsley

3 cups finely chopped
fresh cilantro

2 cups finely chopped
fresh chives

1 cup finely chopped fresh
fenugreek leaves

⅓ cup vegetable oil,
plus 3 tablespoons

1 medium yellow onion,
finely chopped

1 pound lamb loin, cut
into 1-inch cubes

1 teaspoon ground turmeric

4 to 5 cups water

1 cup kidney beans, soaked
in water overnight

4 or 5 whole dried limes,
soaked in water for 1 hour

1 teaspoon salt

1 teaspoon freshly ground
black pepper

Chelo (page 104) or Kateh
(page 22), for serving

WORTH THE WAIT There are a lot of stews in Persian cuisine, and all are served with either *chelo* (Persian Steamed White Rice with saffron; see page 104) or *kateh* (Easy Persian Rice; see page 22). Khoresh-e-Ghormeh Sabzi is one of the more basic Persian stews; it's made with a lots of different herbs, kidney beans, and lamb (if you're vegan, just leave out the lamb). The addition of the dried lime gives a unique tanginess to the dish. If you're using canned kidney beans, drain and rinse them, then add them with dried limes in step 6.

1. Heat a large, dry skillet over low heat, add the parsley, cilantro, chives, and fenugreek, and cook for about 10 minutes, stirring frequently, until the herbs dry out a little. Add ⅓ cup of vegetable oil and cook the herbs, stirring constantly, for about 15 minutes more. Turn off the heat and set the herbs aside.

2. Heat the remaining 3 tablespoons of vegetable oil in a large pot over medium heat. When the oil begins to shimmer, add the onion and sauté until it's golden brown, about 10 minutes. Add the lamb and turmeric to the pot and sauté until the lamb is light brown on all sides, about 5 minutes.

3. Add the water to the pot, increase the heat to high, bring the liquid to a boil, then reduce the heat to medium and simmer the stew for 10 minutes.

4. Drain the kidney beans and add them to the stew. Cover the pot and simmer for 30 minutes, then add the sautéed herbs, cover the pot again, reduce the heat to low, and cook for 1 to 1½ hours. Check on the stew every 30 minutes and add ½ cup more water if the stew seems too dry. Don't add too much water, though, as you want the end result to be thick and hearty.

5. Drain the dried limes, prick them all over with a fork, and add them to the stew, along with the salt and pepper. Simmer for another 15 minutes to infuse the flavors.

6. Serve hot with chelo or Keteh.

BEYOND THE BASICS Drop three ice cubes into the stew 10 minutes before serving, when the stew is still hot. This temperature shock causes all the oil to come to the surface— which tells you the stew has been cooked perfectly. If you like, you can skim off the fat to make the meal a bit lighter.

My Memories

I refused to eat Fesenjan for the first six years of my life because of its dark brown color. Every time my maman made it, I wouldn't even bother to give it a taste. My maman's disci- pline was very effective. She'd say, "That's all we have; eat it or leave it." And there I would be, having plain white rice while the rest of the family would eat the delicious Fesenjan with lots of appetite and excitement, telling me how delicious it was and that I was making a big mistake by opting out.

One day I finally gave in and had some Fesenjan with my first spoonful of rice. I fell in love with it! And to this very day, I regret those six years that I refused to eat this delicious stew.

The key to a great stew is a long cooking time over low heat. The simmering helps to blend all the flavors like instruments in an orchestra: They each have their own individual characteristics one by one, but together, they create magic!

In fact, some Persian stews, including Fesenjan and Ghormeh Sabzi (Persian Herb Stew) taste much better if they are eaten one day after they are cooked, because the flavors blend better as time passes.

POMEGRANATE & WALNUT STEW

Serves 4
Prep: 10 minutes
Cook: 1 hour, 50 minutes

1 pound shelled
unsalted walnuts

1 tablespoon vegetable oil

1 medium yellow onion,
finely chopped

3 cups warm water

1 pound cooked and
mashed pumpkin

6 skinless, bone-in
chicken thighs

1½ cups pomegranate
molasses, divided

2 tablespoons brown
sugar (optional)

1 teaspoon salt

½ teaspoon freshly ground
black pepper

Chelo (page 104),
for serving

WORTH THE WAIT Khoresh-e-Fesenjan is one of the most delicious and diverse stews in Persian cuisine. A little change here or there, and the flavor profile is altered significantly. The pomegranate molasses has a tangy and sour taste, which can be adjusted by adding sugar. The chicken can be left out for a egan version. In some cities in northern Iran, it's made with duck. If you decide to go that way, increase the cooking time in step 3 by 2 hours. And because the walnuts are crushed into fine crumbs, this stew has a velvety and thick texture. Walnut, however, is *garmi* (heating); the addition of *sardi* (cooling) pumpkin will balance it.

1. Using a food processor, grind the walnuts into very fine crumbs. Set aside.

2. Heat the vegetable oil in a large pot over medium heat. When the oil begins to shimmer, add the onion and sauté until it's golden brown, about 10 minutes. Add the crushed walnuts and cook for 5 minutes, stirring constantly, then pour in the water. Increase the heat to medium high, bring the liquid to a boil, then reduce the heat to medium, add the pumpkin and chicken, cover the pot, and simmer for 30 minutes.

3. After 30 minutes, check and see if the chicken is cooked through. When it is, add 1 cup of pomegranate molasses, cover the pot, and simmer for 15 minutes more.

4. Take the chicken thighs out of the stew and place them on a plate. Set them aside.

5. Taste the stew. If it's too sour for your taste, add the brown sugar, if it's not sour enough, add the remaining 1/2 cup of pomegranate molasses.

6. Stir in the salt and pepper, then cover the pot and let the stew simmer for 30 more minutes. If the stew is too thick, add 1 extra cup of water.

7. Add the chicken thighs back into the stew, cover the pot, and simmer for 20 minutes or until the chicken is heated through.

8. Serve hot with chelo.

MAKE IT EASIER If you don't want to cook and mash the pumpkin ahead of time, use canned pumpkin purée instead (one 15-ounce can will do the trick). Just make sure that the only thing in the can is mashed pumpkin; pumpkin pie filling has sugar and spices, which you don't want. You can also use mashed kabocha or butternut squash instead of pumpkin.

GREEN BEAN STEW

خورش لوبیا سبز KHORESH-E-LOOBIA SABZ

Serves 4
Prep: 10 minutes
Cook: 1 hour, 35 minutes

5 tablespoons vegetable oil, divided

2 medium yellow onions, finely chopped

1 pound lamb loin, cut into ½-inch cubes

1 teaspoon ground turmeric

3 cups water

1 pound fresh green beans, trimmed and cut into 2-inch pieces

1 teaspoon salt

1 teaspoon freshly ground black pepper

2 tablespoons bloomed saffron (optional, see page 21)

3 tablespoons tomato paste

4 tablespoons freshly squeezed lemon juice

1 large white potato, peeled and cut into small cubes

Chelo (page 104), for serving

SUBSTITUTION TIP

You can use beef stew meat instead of lamb in this recipe.

WORTH THE WAIT Khoresh-e-Loobia Sabz is common in the Azeri region, in the northwest of Iran. This stew is made with fresh green beans and lamb chunks. Like every stew, it's served in shallow dishes around a big platter of Steamed White Rice (*chelo*), page 104. Many people also top this stew with sautéed potatoes, as I've done in this recipe.

1. Heat 2 tablespoons of vegetable oil in a large pot over medium heat. When the oil begins to shimmer, add the onions and sauté until golden brown, about 10 minutes. Add the lamb and cook until the lamb pieces are light brown on all sides, 5 to 7 minutes. Stir in the turmeric and mix well.

2. Add the water to the pot, cover, and let the stew cook for about 30 minutes until the lamb is halfway cooked. The meat will be light brown but not completely tender.

3. Add the green beans to the pot, cover, and cook for another 30 minutes, until both the beans and the lamb are tender. Check the stew occasionally to make sure there is enough water in the pot, and add more as needed.

4. Stir in the salt, pepper, bloomed saffron (if using), and tomato paste. Stir until the tomato paste is completely dissolved in the stew, then add the lemon juice, cover the pot, and turn off the heat while you make the potatoes.

5. Heat the remaining 3 tablespoons of vegetable oil in a small saucepan over medium heat. When the oil begins to shimmer, add the potato and sauté until it is golden brown and tender, 10 to 20 minutes.

6. Serve the stew hot with chelo, topped with the potatoes.

ZUCCHINI STEW

خورش کدو سبز KHORESH-E-KADOO

Serves 4
Prep: 10 minutes
Cook: 1 hour

5 tablespoons vegetable
oil, divided

4 zucchini, peeled and halved
lengthwise, then cut into
thin half-moons

6 skinless, bone-in
chicken thighs

1 onion, finely chopped

1 teaspoon ground turmeric

½ teaspoon freshly ground
black pepper

2 tablespoons tomato paste

2½ cups water

1 teaspoon salt

2 tablespoons freshly
squeezed lemon juice

Chelo (page 104),
for serving

WORTH THE WAIT Khoresh-e-Kadoo is one of the easiest Persian stews you can make. It usually calls for chicken thighs, but some families make it with chunks of beef instead. The addition of lemon juice makes the stew a little bit sour, which perfectly complements the flavors of zucchini and tomato paste. A word of warning: Zucchini can get mushy if cooked for too long, so make sure to watch it closely.

1. Heat 2 tablespoons of vegetable oil in a large pot over medium heat. When the oil begins to shimmer, add the zucchini and cook just until golden, 6 to 8 minutes. Transfer the zucchini to a plate and set it aside.

2. In the same pot, heat 2 tablespoons of vegetable oil over medium heat. When the oil begins to shimmer, add the chicken thighs and cook until they are browned on both sides, 6 to 8 minutes. Transfer the chicken to a plate and set it aside.

3. Heat the remaining 1 tablespoon of vegetable oil in the same pot over medium heat and sauté the onion until golden brown, about 10 minutes. Add the turmeric and black pepper. Stir well. Add the tomato paste and water. Keep stirring until the tomato paste is dissolved.

4. Increase the heat to medium high and bring the stew to a boil, then reduce the heat to medium and add the chicken thighs. Cover the pot and cook for 20 minutes or until the chicken thighs are completely cooked.

5. Add the zucchini, salt, and lemon juice to the pot. Simmer uncovered for another 10 minutes or until the zucchini is heated through.

6. Serve with chelo.

SUBSTITUTION TIP For a vegan version, use mushrooms instead of chicken thighs and add them after the stew starts boiling in step 4. The cooking time will be reduced to 30 minutes, as there is no need to sauté the mushrooms first.

CELERY STEW

خورش کرفس KHORESH-E-KARAFS

Serves 4
Prep: 15 minutes
Cook: 1 hour, 50 minutes

4 tablespoons vegetable oil, divided

1½ cups finely chopped fresh parsley

1 cup finely chopped fresh mint

7 celery stalks, cut into ½-inch pieces

1 large yellow onion, finely chopped

1 pound beef loin, cut into ½-inch chunks

3 to 4 cups water

3 whole dried Persian limes

1 tablespoon bloomed saffron (see page 21)

1 teaspoon salt

1 teaspoon freshly ground black pepper

Chelo (page 104), for serving

WORTH THE WAIT One thing I love about rice and stew is that you can easily adjust the amounts on your plate. I always like to have more stew than rice, because I like to eat my *tahdig* (the golden crust at the bottom of the pot of steamed rice) with some extra stew. Khoresh-e-Karafs is a very nutritious stew made of celery, lamb, and herbs. The dried lime gives it a tangy-sweet flavor, and fresh mint imparts a lovely brightness. This stew can be made with either lamb or beef. Or for a vegan version, leave the meat out and add a can of drained and rinsed kidney beans with the dried limes in step 3.

1. Heat 2 tablespoons of vegetable oil in a large pot over medium heat. When the oil begins to simmer, add the parsley, mint, and celery and sauté for 3 minutes. Immediately transfer the herbs and celery to a plate and set aside.

2. Heat the remaining 2 tablespoons of vegetable oil in the same pot over medium heat. When the oil begins to shimmer, add the onion and sauté until it's translucent, about 5 minutes, then add the beef and sauté until it is light brown on all sides, 3 to 5 minutes.

3. Add the water and bring it to a boil, then reduce the heat to low, cover the pot, and let the stew simmer for 20 minutes. Add the sautéed herbs and celery. Cover and simmer until the meat is fully cooked and the celery is soft, about 40 to 50 minutes.

4. Prick the dried limes all over with a fork, drop them in the stew, cover the pot, and cook for another 20 minutes to infuse the flavor. Stir in the bloomed saffron, salt, and pepper. Cover and cook for 10 minutes more.

5. Serve hot with chelo.

SUBSTITUTION TIP In this recipe, the dried limes can be replaced with ⅓ cup freshly squeezed lemon juice.

CARROT STEW

خورش هویج KHORESH-E-HAVIJ

Serves 4
Prep: 10 minutes
Cook: 1 hour, 40 minutes

3 tablespoons vegetable oil, divided

1 medium yellow onion, finely chopped

1 pound beef loin, cut into ½-inch cubes

1 teaspoon ground turmeric

2 cups water

5 large carrots, peeled, quartered lengthwise, and cut into 2-inch pieces

2 tablespoons tomato paste

¾ cup Persian dried plums

1 teaspoon salt

1 teaspoon freshly ground black pepper

Chelo (page 104) or Kateh (page 22), for serving

WORTH THE WAIT Khoresh-e-Havij is one of the most underappreciated Persian stews. The main ingredient is carrots and the protein is beef loin. For extra flavor, Persian dried plums are added, which have a nice orange color and a tart flavor. You can buy them from Middle Eastern or Russian supermarkets, or online. You can also use lamb stew meat instead of beef. And for a vegan version, substitute sliced mushrooms, adding them when the carrots are half cooked.

1. Heat 2 tablespoons of vegetable oil in a large pot over medium heat. When the oil begins to shimmer, add the onion and sauté until it's golden brown, about 10 minutes. Add the beef and cook until it is light brown on all sides, 5 to 7 minutes. Stir in the turmeric and mix well.

2. Add the water to the pot, increase the heat to high, and bring the liquid to a boil. Then reduce the heat to medium, cover the pot, and let the stew cook for about 30 minutes, until the beef is cooked halfway through. The meat will be browned but not completely tender.

3. Meanwhile, heat the remaining 1 tablespoon of vegetable oil in a medium skillet and sauté the carrots for about 7 minutes, until they soften. Add the carrots to the stew, cover the pot, and cook for 40 more minutes, until the beef is completely tender.

4. Add the tomato paste and Persian dried plums and stir until the tomato paste is completely dissolved in the stew. Add the salt and pepper, cover the pot, and cook for another 15 minutes to marry the flavors.

5. Serve hot with chelo or kateh.

INGREDIENT TIP Soak the dried plums in warm water for 30 minutes before adding them to the stew. This will make them softer.

SPLIT CHICKPEA STEW

خورش قیمه KHORESH-E-GHEIMEH

Serves 4
Prep: 10 minutes
Cook: 1 hour, 30 minutes

6 tablespoons vegetable oil, divided

1 medium yellow onion, finely chopped

4 tablespoons split chickpeas, rinsed and drained

12 ounces beef loin, cut into ½-inch cubes

1 teaspoon ground turmeric

2 cups water

4 whole Persian dried limes

1 teaspoon salt

½ teaspoon cayenne pepper

2 tablespoons tomato paste

1 large white potato, cut into shoestring strips

½ teaspoon ground cinnamon

3 tablespoons rosewater

Chelo (page 104), for serving

WORTH THE WAIT You will find Khoresh-e-Gheimeh on the menu at most Persian restaurants. This stew is made with split chickpeas, which may be labeled dal, daal, or toor dhal in Indian or Middle Eastern grocery stores. Khoresh-e-Gheimeh can be topped with fried potatoes—as in this recipe—or fried or grilled eggplant.

1. Heat 2 tablespoons of vegetable oil in a large pot over medium heat. When the oil begins to shimmer, add the onion and split chickpeas and sauté for 10 minutes, stirring constantly, or until the onion is golden brown. Stir in the beef and sauté until it is light brown on all sides, 5 to 7 minutes. Add the turmeric to the pot and mix well to coat the beef pieces.

2. Add the water to the pot and bring it to a boil, then reduce the heat to low and simmer until the beef is completely tender, 40 to 50 minutes.

3. Pierce the Persian dried limes all over with a fork and add them to the stew. Add the salt, cayenne, and tomato paste. Cook for 10 minutes more.

4. Meanwhile, heat the remaining 4 tablespoons of vegetable oil in a large skillet over medium heat. Fry the potato until it is golden and crispy and cooked through, 4 to 6 minutes. Transfer the fried potatoes to a paper towel–lined plate and set it aside.

5. Add the cinnamon and rosewater to the stew, and simmer on low for an additional 10 minutes.

6. Serve the stew in shallow bowls, topped with some fried potato. Serve with chelo.

SUBSTITUTION TIP To make the stew with eggplants, leave out the potato. Peel three Chinese eggplants (the long, thin ones), cut them in half lengthwise, and slice them into thin half-moons. Sauté the eggplants in 4 tablespoons of vegetable oil until they are golden brown on both sides, then place them on top of the stew in the pot. Let the stew simmer for an extra 10 minutes, then continue with step 5.

CHICKEN WITH TOMATO SAUCE

خوراک مرغ KHORAK-E-MORGH

Serves 6
Prep: 15 minutes
Cook: 1 hour, 10 minutes

5 tablespoons vegetable oil, divided

2 tablespoons unsalted butter (optional)

6 bone-in, skin-on chicken thighs

4 tablespoons bloomed saffron (see page 21), divided

1 medium yellow onion, finely chopped

3 carrots, peeled, halved lengthwise, and cut into 2-inch pieces

2 green bell peppers, stemmed, seeded, and cut into 1-inch squares

½ teaspoon ground turmeric

2 tablespoons tomato paste

1½ cups water

1 teaspoon salt

½ teaspoon cayenne pepper

Chelo (page 104), Kateh (page 22), or Barberry & Saffron Rice (page 110), for serving

WORTH THE WAIT Khorak-e-Morgh is a flavor-packed meal of chicken, vegetables, and spices that can be served on its own with some fresh bread or Kateh (page 22). The traditional way, however, is to serve it with Barberry & Saffron Rice (page 110). You can use different cuts of chicken in this dish, such as drumsticks or breasts, but I like the thighs because they have more flavor. Like most stews, you can freeze the leftovers and thaw and reheat them another day.

1. Heat 3 tablespoons of vegetable oil in a large skillet over medium-high heat. Add the butter (if using), let it melt, then put the chicken thighs in the pan, skin-side down. Pour 2 tablespoons of bloomed saffron around the pan and tilt it a little so the saffron runs under the chicken thighs. Fry the chicken for 7 minutes or until the skin is golden and crispy. Turn the chicken thighs over and fry the other side another 5 minutes. Take the chicken thighs out of the pan and set them aside on a plate.

2. Heat the remaining 2 tablespoons of vegetable oil in the same skillet over medium heat and sauté the onion until it's translucent, about 5 minutes. Add the carrots and peppers and sauté for 5 minutes more or until they begin to soften. Add the turmeric and tomato paste and sauté until the tomato paste darkens, 1 to 2 minutes.

3. Add the water, salt, cayenne, and the remaining 2 table-spoons of bloomed saffron. Stir until the tomato paste is completely dissolved in the water. Place the chicken thighs on top of the vegetables and spoon some of the sauce over them.

4. Bring the sauce to a simmer, cover the skillet, and let it cook for 40 to 45 minutes, until the chicken is completely cooked. Spoon the sauce over the chicken thighs every 15 minutes to keep them moist.

5. Serve hot with chelo, kateh, or Barberry & Saffron Rice.

SUBSTITUTION TIP Plain tomato sauce is a great substitute here for the tomato paste. Reduce the amount of water to ¾ cup and add one 8-ounce can of tomato sauce after adding the turmeric. Then just follow the recipe.

SAFFRON CHICKEN

مرغ زعفرانی MORGH-E-ZAFERANI

Serves 6
Prep: 10 minutes
Cook: 1 hour, 5 minutes

4 tablespoons vegetable oil, divided

6 bone-in, skin-on chicken thighs

8 tablespoons bloomed saffron (see page 21), divided

1 medium yellow onion, finely chopped

½ teaspoon ground turmeric

½ teaspoon ground cinnamon

2 green bell peppers, stemmed, seeded, and cut into 1-inch squares

1 cup water

1 teaspoon salt

½ teaspoon freshly ground black pepper

Chelo (page 104), Kateh (page 22), or Herbs & Rice (page 106), for serving

WORTH THE WAIT Morgh-e-Zaferani is made with lots of onions and saffron. It can be enjoyed on its own or with Herbs & Rice (page 106). Because there's a lot of saffron in this dish, Morgh-e Zaferani counts as a fancy food for gatherings and parties.

1. Heat 2 tablespoons of vegetable oil in a large skillet over medium-high heat. When the oil begins to shimmer, place the chicken thighs in the skillet, skin-side down. Pour 4 tablespoons of bloomed saffron around the pan and tilt it a little so the saffron runs under the chicken thighs. Cook for 5 minutes, until the skin is golden. Turn the chicken thighs over and cook the other side for another 5 minutes. Take the chicken thighs out of the pan and set them aside on a plate.

2. Heat the remaining 2 tablespoons of vegetable oil in the same skillet over medium heat and sauté the onion until it is golden brown, about 10 minutes. Add the turmeric and cinnamon. Stir well. Add the bell peppers and stir.

3. Place the chicken thighs in the pan with the onion and bell peppers and pour the remaining 4 tablespoons of bloomed saffron over the top. Add the water, salt, and pepper to the skillet.

4. Cover the skillet and cook for 40 to 45 minutes, turning the chicken thighs every 15 minutes, until the chicken is cooked completely.

5. Serve hot with chelo, kateh, or Herbs & Rice.

MAKE IT EASIER To cook this dish in the oven, preheat the oven to 400°F. After step 1, coat an oven-safe dish with non-stick cooking spray, place the onion and pepper in the bottom, sprinkle on the turmeric, salt, and freshly ground black pepper, then place the chicken on top and pour the bloomed saffron over each chicken thigh. Add the water and roast in the oven for 45 minutes, until the chicken is completely cooked.

LAMB SHANKS

خوراک ماهیچه KHORAK-E-MAHICHEH

Serves 6
Prep: 20 minutes
Cook: 2 hours

2 pounds lamb shanks

2 large yellow onions,
finely chopped, divided

2½ cups water

3 garlic cloves, minced

1 teaspoon ground turmeric

3 tablespoons vegetable oil

2 tablespoons tomato paste

1 teaspoon ground cinnamon

1 teaspoon salt

1 teaspoon cayenne pepper

½ teaspoon ground cumin

2 tablespoons bloomed
saffron (see page 21)

2 tablespoons freshly
squeezed lemon juice

Chelo (page 104) or Dill &
Fava Bean Rice (page 108),
for serving

WORTH THE WAIT Khorak-e-Mahicheh is lamb shanks cooked in a tomato sauce for a long time, until they are tender and flavorful. For this dish, you can use either bone-in lamb shanks or boneless lamb loin, but I prefer bone-in lamb because it tends to be more flavorful. If you are using boneless lamb loin, cut it into 3-inch chunks and shorten the cooking time by almost 30 minutes. You can also make this dish with a saffron sauce. Simply leave out the tomato paste and increase the amount of bloomed saffron to 5 tablespoons.

1. In a large pot, combine the lamb shanks, half of the chopped onions, the water, garlic, and turmeric. Cover the pot and cook the lamb over medium heat for 1 to 1½ hours, until the lamb is tender and cooked through.

2. About 10 minutes before the lamb is done cooking, heat the vegetable oil in a large skillet over medium heat. Sauté the remaining chopped onion until it's translucent and a little bit golden, 5 to 7 minutes. Add the tomato paste and sauté for 3 minutes, then add the cinnamon, salt, cayenne, and cumin and cook for 2 more minutes, stirring constantly. Remove the skillet from the heat and cover it with a lid to keep warm.

3. When the lamb is done cooking, take the pieces out of the pot and add them to the tomato paste and onion in the skillet. Using tongs, turn the lamb pieces so all sides are smothered with spices.

4. Place a colander on a large bowl and pour the juice from the lamb through the colander to strain out the onion and garlic. Place the skillet with the lamb and onions over low heat and pour in the strained lamb juices. Stir well until the tomato paste is dissolved.

5. Turn the heat up to medium and bring the juices to a simmer. Add the bloomed saffron and lemon juice and simmer the lamb shanks in the sauce for 30 minutes.

6. Serve warm with chelo or Dill & Fava Bean Rice.

MAKE IT EASIER To complete step 1 in a slow cooker, simply combine the lamb, onion, garlic, turmeric, and 3 to 4 cups of water and cook on low for 8 hours, then continue with step 2.

STEAMED WHITE RICE

 چلو CHELO

Serves 4
Prep: 10 minutes
Cook: 50 minutes

6½ cups water, divided

2 cups long-grain white rice, such as basmati, rinsed and drained

1½ teaspoons salt

6 tablespoons vegetable oil, divided

1 tablespoon bloomed saffron (see page 21)

Thin bread for the bottom of the pot (lavash or a flour tortilla works well)

VEGAN This method for steaming rice creates a perfect result every time—tender, fluffy, separated grains with the famous Persian tahdig (crispy golden crust) at the bottom of the pot. It is an ideal accompaniment for all sorts of stews, vegetable, and meat dishes, either as is or adorned with a tablespoon or two of bloomed saffron.Once you perfect this recipe, try using different types of bread or mashed starchy vegetables like potatoes for the tahdig.

1. Pour 6 cups of water into a large nonstick pot and bring it to a boil over high heat. Add the rinsed rice and salt. Let it boil uncovered for almost 10 minutes. Check one grain by pressing it between your thumb and index finger; you should be able to break the grain but it should still be firm.

2. Place a fine-mesh colander in the sink, drain the rice, and set it aside.

3. Put the empty pot back on the stove over medium heat. Make sure the bottom of the pot is dry. Heat 3 tablespoons of vegetable oil in the pot. Add the bloomed saffron and place the thin bread in the pot so it covers the bottom entirely.

4. Scoop the rice back into the pot. Push most of the rice toward the middle of the pot, shaping it into a mound. Pour the remaining 1/2 cup of water around the edges of the pot. Using the edge of a spatula, make five holes in the surface of the rice to let the steam escape. Wrap the lid in a clean towel and put it on the pot. Let the rice cook for 30 minutes, until the steam starts to escape.

5. Pour the remaining 3 tablespoons of vegetable oil over the rice, cover, and steam for 10 minutes more.

6. Serve warm with any stew.

WHY IT WORKS The clean towel wrapping the lid will absorb the steam perfectly and won't let it drip back into the rice and make it sticky. Making the holes in the rice will also vent the steam and prevent the rice from being sticky.

HERBS & RICE

سبزی پلو SABZI POLO

Serves 4
Prep: 15 minutes
Cook: 50 minutes

6½ cups water, divided

2 cups long-grain white rice, such as basmati, rinsed and drained

1½ teaspoons salt

1 cup finely chopped fresh dill

½ cup finely chopped fresh chives

½ cup finely chopped fresh cilantro

1 cup finely chopped fresh parsley

7 tablespoons vegetable oil, divided

4 whole romaine lettuce leaves

VEGAN Sabzi Polo is made with long-grain rice and herbs and a crispy romaine lettuce crust. If you like, you can use thin bread (such as lavash) instead of lettuce for the crust. Simply place the bread at the bottom of the pot when the oil is hot. Because of all the herbs, this dish is very fragrant, nutritious, and bright green in color. It is traditionally served with fish.

1. Pour 6 cups of water into a large nonstick pot and bring it to a boil over high heat. Add the rinsed rice and salt. Let it boil for about 10 minutes. Check one grain by pressing it between your thumb and index finger; you should be able to break the grain but it should still be firm.

2. Place a fine-mesh colander in the sink, drain the rice, and set it aside.

3. Place the empty pot back on the stove over medium heat. Make sure the bottom of the pot is dry. Add the dill, chives, cilantro, and parsley to the rice in the colander and mix well.

4. Heat 3 tablespoons of vegetable oil in the pot and place the romaine lettuce leaves in the pot so they cover the bottom completely.

5. Scoop the rice and herbs back into the pot. Bring most of the rice to the middle, shaping it into a mound. Using the edge of a spatula, make five holes in the surface of the rice to let the steam escape. Pour the remaining ½ cup of water around the edges of the pot. Wrap the lid in a clean towel and put it on the pot. Let the rice cook for 30 minutes, until the steam starts to escape.

6. Pour the remaining 4 tablespoons of vegetable oil over the rice, cover, and steam for 10 minutes more. Serve warm.

COOKING TIP Check the rice after the final 10 minutes in step 6. If it is undercooked, add ⅓ cup more water, cover, and cook for an additional 10 minutes. Don't add too much water, as it will make the rice sticky.

DILL & FAVA BEAN RICE

شوید باقالی پلو SHEVID BAGHALI POLO

Serves 4
Prep: 20 minutes
Cook: 1 hour, 20 minutes

1 cup shelled fresh fava beans

2 cups finely chopped
fresh dill

4 tablespoons bloomed
saffron (see page 21), divided

6½ cups water, divided

2 cups long-grain white rice,
such as basmati, rinsed
and drained

1½ teaspoons salt

6 tablespoons vegetable
oil, divided

Thin bread for the bottom of
the pot (lavash works best)

VEGAN, WORTH THE WAIT Fava beans have a lovely nutty flavor and aroma, and they give a nice crunch to each spoonful of this dish. Shevid Baghali Polo is typically served with Saffron Chicken (page 100) or Lamb Shanks (page 102) and is very common at Persian weddings and festive gatherings.

1. Mix the fava beans, dill, and 2 tablespoons of bloomed saffron in a large bowl. Set aside.

2. Pour 6 cups of water into a large nonstick pot and bring it to a boil over high heat. Add the rinsed rice and salt. Let it boil for almost 10 minutes. Check one grain with your fingers by pressing it between your thumb and index finger; you should be able to break the grain but it should still be firm.

3. Place a fine-mesh colander in the sink, drain the rice, and set it aside.

4. Place the empty pot back on the stove over medium heat. Make sure the bottom of the pot is dry. Heat 3 tablespoons of vegetable oil in the pot, add 2 tablespoons of bloomed saffron, and place the thin bread in the pot so it covers the bottom entirely.

5. Layer one third of the rice in the bottom of the pot and top with one third of the fava bean mixture. Repeat the layers until all the rice and fava beans are back in the pot. Bring most of the rice to the middle of the pot, shaping it into a mound. Using the edge of a spatula, make five holes in the surface of the rice to let the steam escape.

6. Pour the remaining ½ cup of water around the edges of the pot. Wrap the lid in a clean towel and put it on the pot. Let the rice cook for 30 minutes, until the steam starts to escape.

7. Pour the remaining 3 tablespoons of vegetable oil over the rice, cover, reduce the heat to low, and steam for 40 minutes, until the fava beans are cooked completely. Serve warm.

SUBSTITUTION TIP You can use frozen fava beans instead of fresh—just make sure they are completely thawed. You can also use 1½ cups dried dill instead of 2 cups fresh dill. The steps are the same.

BARBERRY & SAFFRON RICE

 زرشک پلو ZERESHK POLO

Serves 4
Prep: 20 minutes
Cook: 5 minutes

4 tablespoons barberries,
rinsed and dried

1 tablespoon water

1½ tablespoons vegetable oil

1 tablespoon sugar

5 tablespoons bloomed
saffron (see page 21), divided

1 recipe Chelo (page 104)

VEGAN, QUICK & EASY Zereshk Polo is a layered dish of plain white rice, saffron rice, and barberries. Barberries are small, red, sour berries. They are sautéed with vegetable oil and sometimes sugar to balance their pungency, according to the taste of the cook. Zereshk Polo is usually served with Chicken with Tomato Sauce (page 98). This is a very common dish for fancy Persian gatherings, especially weddings.

1. Combine the barberries, water, vegetable oil, sugar, and 2 tablespoons of bloomed saffron in a small saucepan. Let it sit for 10 minutes, then place the pan over medium-low heat. Cook the barberries until they are bright red and shiny and all the water has evaporated, about 5 to 7 minutes, stirring occasionally. Remove the pan from the heat and set it aside.

2. Scoop 1 cup of chelo into a medium bowl and mix it with the remaining 3 tablespoons of bloomed saffron. Spoon half of the remaining chelo onto a large platter, then layer it with half of the saffron rice and half of the barberry mixture. Layer with the remaining chelo and finish with the remaining saffron rice and barberries.

3. Serve warm.

COOKING TIP If the barberries are bright red and shiny in step 2 but there is still water in the pan, just spoon out the water. Don't cook the barberries too much, as they can get dark and hard to chew. Taste the barberries before serving the dish. If they are too sour, add ½ teaspoon sugar.

OKRA STEW

خورش بامیه KHORESH-E-BAMIEH

Serves 4
Prep: 10 minutes
Cook: 1 hour, 35 minutes

2 tablespoons vegetable oil

1 medium yellow onion, finely chopped

1 teaspoon ground turmeric

12 ounces beef loin, cut into ½-inch cubes

2½ cups water

2 garlic cloves, minced

12 ounces fresh okra, rinsed and stemmed

2 tablespoons tomato paste

2 tablespoons freshly squeezed lemon juice

1 teaspoon salt

1 teaspoon freshly ground black pepper

Chelo (page 104), for serving

WORTH THE WAIT Khoresh-e-Bamieh is a stew made of fresh okra, a vegetable that has an eggplant-like flavor when cooked. I like to use beef in my version of this Persian classic, but for a vegan stew you can leave out the meat and use only okra. The green okra and red gravy makes a beautiful contrast.

1. Heat the vegetable oil in a large pot over medium heat. When the oil begins to shimmer, add the onion and sauté until it's golden brown, about 10 minutes. Mix in the turmeric, then add the beef and cook until it is light brown on all sides, 5 to 7 minutes.

2. Pour in the water, increase the heat to high, and bring the liquid to a boil. Then reduce the heat to medium, cover the pot, and let the stew cook until the beef is completely tender, about 50 minutes.

3. When the beef is tender, add the garlic to the pot, cover, and cook for another 10 minutes.

4. Add the okra and tomato paste and stir until the tomato paste is dissolved in the stew. Cover and cook the stew for 20 minutes more, until the okra is tender but not falling apart.

5. Stir in the lemon juice, salt, and pepper. Taste the stew and add more salt, if needed.

6. Serve hot with chelo.

INGREDIENT TIP Be careful to remove only the stems from the okra—do not cut off the whole tops. If you cut off too much of these little vegetables, the seeds will escape from the pods and make the stew slimy.

6 CHICKEN, MEAT & FISH

STUFFED ROASTED CHICKEN

مرغ شکم پر MORGH-E-SHEKAM POR

Serves 6
Prep: 20 minutes
Cook: 1 hour, 30 minutes

1 whole chicken

Nonstick cooking spray

3 large carrots, peeled
and halved lengthwise

3 medium yellow
onions, divided

4 garlic cloves, minced

3 tablespoons chopped
unsalted walnuts

4 tablespoons barberries,
rinsed and dried

1 tablespoon pomegranate
molasses

1 tablespoons sugar

1 tablespoon tomato paste

2 teaspoons ground
turmeric, divided

2 teaspoons ground
cinnamon, divided

1 teaspoon cayenne pepper

3 tablespoons olive oil,
plus ¼ cup

3 tablespoons bloomed
saffron (optional; see page 21)

WORTH THE WAIT The stuffing for this classic roast chicken dish can be different in each family, from simple onions, tomatoes, carrots, and bell peppers, to walnuts, plums, and barberries. The recipe here is our family favorite.

1. Preheat the oven to 350°F.

2. Rinse the chicken and pat it dry using paper towels. Make sure the chicken is very clean and dry, especially on the inside. Using your fingers, gently open the space between the skin and the meat; try not to tear the skin. Set the chicken aside.

3. Spray an ovenproof dish or roasting pan with nonstick cooking spray and place the carrots on the bottom. Cut 2 of the onions into quarters and place them around the carrots. Set aside.

4. Chop the remaining 1 onion very finely and place it in a medium bowl. Add the garlic, walnuts, barberries, pomegranate molasses, sugar, tomato paste, 1 teaspoon of turmeric, 1 teaspoon of cinnamon, the cayenne, and 3 tablespoons of olive oil. Mix very well until all the ingredients are combined and coated in olive oil and spices. Add 1 more tablespoon of olive oil, if the mixture looks too dry.

5. In a small bowl, mix together the remaining 1 teaspoon of turmeric and 1 teaspoon of cinnamon, the remaining ¼ cup of olive oil, and the bloomed saffron (if using). Using your hands, rub this spiced oil underneath and over the top of the chicken skin; try not to tear the skin.

6. Fill the cavity of the chicken with the onion-walnut mixture. Tie the chicken legs together using a thick thread and place the chicken on top of the carrots and onions in the baking dish. Tuck the wings under so they won't burn.

7. Roast the chicken in the oven for 1 hour, then baste the chicken all over with the pan juices, using a brush, and roast for 30 minutes more, basting every 10 minutes.

8. Take the chicken out of the oven, cut the thread around the legs, and spoon out the stuffing into a serving bowl. Carve the chicken and serve it warm with the vegetables and stuffing on the side.

COOKING TIP Rubbing the spice mixture under the skin might seem like a difficult job, but the skin lifts quite easily, and this gives the chicken extra flavor. Adding olive oil to the spices makes them easier to rub and keeps the chicken juicier.

CHICKEN KABOBS

جوجه کباب — JOOJEH KABOB

Serves 6
Prep: 15 minutes,
plus 6 hours to marinate
Cook: 30 minutes

2 whole boneless, skinless
chicken breasts, cut into
2½-inch cubes

3 medium yellow onions,
thinly sliced

2 green bell peppers,
stemmed, seeded, and cut
into 2-inch pieces

1½ cups plain Greek yogurt

Juice of 1 large lemon

4 tablespoons vegetable oil

5 tablespoons bloomed
saffron (see page 21)

1 teaspoon freshly ground
black pepper

2 teaspoons salt

4 medium tomatoes,
cut in half

8 medium jalapeño peppers

Bread or Chelo (page 104),
for serving

COOKING TIP You can
bake these kabobs in the
oven at 375°F for 25 to
30 minutes. Then broil the
chicken pieces until golden.

WORTH THE WAIT For Joojeh Kabob, chicken breasts
are cut into small chunks, smothered in a saffron and
yogurt sauce, and left to marinate at least 6 hours to
absorb all the flavor. The kabobs are then cooked on
the grill and served with grilled tomatoes and some
rice on the side. Once you get the hang of it, it'll soon
become a weekday favorite.

1. Place the chicken in a large bowl. Add the onions and bell
peppers, and combine well using your hands. In a separate
bowl, use a fork to mix together the yogurt, lemon juice,
vegetable oil, bloomed saffron, and pepper. Add the yogurt
mixture to the chicken mixture, and stir everything together
using a large spoon. Cover the bowl with plastic wrap and
refrigerate for at least 6 hours or overnight.

2. To make the kabobs, preheat a charcoal or gas grill to
medium high. Take the chicken pieces out of the marinade.
Discard the onions and bell peppers (or cook them in another
dish). Thread the chicken onto metal skewers and place them
on the grill.

3. Grill the chicken kabobs on one side until golden, then turn
all the skewers to cook another side. When that side is also
golden, turn the skewers again. Repeat until all the chicken
pieces are golden brown on all four sides and are cooked completely, 10 to 15 minutes total. Sprinkle the salt on the kabobs.

4. Thread the tomatoes and jalapeños onto metal skewers.
Grill the vegetables until they are tender and their skins are
a bit wrinkled, about 15 minutes total.

5. Serve the chicken kabobs and vegetables warm with bread
or chelo.

HOSSEINI KABOBS

 كباب حسینی KABOB HOSSEINI

Serves 4
Prep: 20 minutes
Cook: 1 hour, 30 minutes

1 pound flank steak, cut into 2-inch cubes

2 medium yellow onions, divided

1 teaspoon salt

1 teaspoon freshly ground black pepper

1 teaspoon ground turmeric

2 tablespoons olive oil

12 cherry tomatoes

1 bell pepper, stemmed, seeded, and cut into 1-inch squares

½ cup water

Fresh bread or Kateh (page 22), for serving

WORTH THE WAIT Did you know you can cook kabobs on the stove top? In this recipe, lean flank steak is cut into small pieces and threaded onto skewers with vegetables, then cooked in a large pan for 1½ to 2 hours. This long cooking time means that the beef cooks in its own juice, resulting in some of the most tender beef you will ever have. Though the kabobs can be cooked right away, they'll be even more delicious if you let the beef marinate in the refrigerator for 3 to 4 hours before cooking.

1. Place the flank steak pieces in a large bowl. Grate one of the onions over the top and add the salt, pepper, turmeric, and olive oil. Mix thoroughly until well combined.

2. Alternate threading the steak pieces and cherry tomatoes onto wooden skewers. Set aside.

3. Heat a large nonstick skillet over medium heat. Thinly slice the remaining onion and place the slices on the bottom of the pan. Arrange the skewers on top of the onions and sprinkle on the bell pepper pieces. Pour the water into the pan and cover it with a lid. Let the kabobs cook for 1½ hours, until the beef pieces are browned and tender. If the beef is not fully cooked when the timer goes off, add ⅓ cup more water and cook for another 30 minutes.

4. Serve warm with some fresh bread or kateh.

BEYOND THE BASICS Add just a little freshly squeezed lemon juice after putting the skewers in the pan. Lemon juice will help the beef cook faster.

BEEF PAN KABOBS

کباب تابه ای KABOB TABEH-I

Serves 4
Prep: 20 minutes
Cook: 40 minutes

1 medium yellow onion

1 pound very lean ground beef
(less than 15% fat)

1 teaspoon ground turmeric

1 teaspoon salt

½ teaspoon freshly ground
black pepper

2 tablespoons vegetable
oil, divided

2 medium tomatoes,
cut into quarters

Chelo (page 104) or Kateh
(page 22), for serving

2 teaspoons sumac or fresh
lemon wedges, for serving

WORTH THE WAIT Kabob Tabeh-i is an easy way to make kabobs, because you don't need to marinate the meat beforehand and you don't need a grill. They're made of lean ground beef, grated onion, salt, pepper, and turmeric. What could be simpler? This dish is generally served with a dash of sumac, a red spice that has a tangy taste. It can be found in Asian, Arab, and Middle Eastern supermarkets. If sumac is not available, squeeze some fresh lemon juice on the kabobs just before serving.

1. Grate the onion, then squeeze it well in a clean kitchen towel or place it in a fine-mesh colander and press it with the back of a wooden spoon to extract as much liquid as possible. Discard the excess water.

2. Place the ground beef in a large bowl and add the grated onion, turmeric, salt, and pepper. Use your hands to mix everything together, then continue kneading the mixture until the meat sticks together, forming a ball.

3. Coat the bottom of a medium skillet with 1 tablespoon of vegetable oil. Wet your hands a little with water, then place the beef mixture in the pan and use your hands to spread it all the way to the edges of the skillet. Using a spatula, divide the mixture into strips.

4. Place the skillet over medium heat and cover it with a lid. When the meat starts to release its juice (after 15 to 20 minutes), uncover the pan and let the juice evaporate. When all the juice has evaporated and one side of the meat is brown, flip the strips using a spatula and cook the other sides until brown, 5 to 10 minutes. Remove the skillet from the heat.

5. In a medium skillet, heat the remaining 1 tablespoon of vegetable oil and sauté the tomatoes until they release their juices and the skins begin to caramelize, 5 to 10 minutes.

6. Serve the kabobs warm with the sautéed tomatoes, chelo or kateh, and some sumac or lemon juice.

COOKING TIP **To knead the beef mixture, grab the whole mixture in your hands and drop it back in the bowl 40 times. This will make the meat stick together.**

LAMB KABOBS

کباب چنجه KABOB CHENJEH

Serves 4
Prep: 15 minutes,
plus overnight to marinate
Cook: 30 minutes

2 pounds lamb sirloin, cut
into 1-inch cubes

2 medium yellow
onions, grated

⅓ cup freshly squeezed
lemon juice

1 teaspoon freshly ground
black pepper

2 tablespoons bloomed
saffron (see page 21)

¼ cup olive oil

1 teaspoon salt

2 teaspoons sumac or fresh
lemon wedges, for serving

Chelo (page 104) or fresh
warm bread, for serving

BEYOND THE BASICS

**Make vegetable skewers
with three halved tomatoes
and six jalapeño peppers
to serve with the lamb
kabobs. Just thread the
veggies on metal skewers
and cook them on the grill
or in the oven until tender
and lightly charred.**

WORTH THE WAIT Kabob Chenjeh may be what comes to mind when you think of Persian cuisine—delicious pieces of lamb sirloin marinated in onion, lemon juice, and spices, then threaded on skewers and cooked on a grill. Marinating the lamb for at least 12 hours will make the meat cook faster and also give it a lot of flavor. Add three peeled and sliced kiwi fruit to the marinade to make the kabobs even more tender.

1. Place the lamb pieces in a large bowl. Add the grated onions, lemon juice, pepper, bloomed saffron, and olive oil. Mix everything together very well using a large spoon. Make sure the lamb pieces are covered with olive oil and onions. Cover the bowl and marinate the lamb in the refrigerator for at least 12 hours.

2. Preheat a charcoal or gas grill to medium high and thread the lamb pieces onto metal skewers. Place the skewers on the grill and cook until one side is browned, 6 to 8 minutes. Grill the kabobs for a total of 25 to 30 minutes, turning the skewers every 5 minutes to make sure they cook evenly. (The time can be shorter if the lamb pieces are smaller.) When the meat is thoroughly browned and cooked through, remove the kabobs from the grill and sprinkle them with the salt. If an outdoor grill is not an option, preheat the oven to 425°F. Line a baking sheet with aluminum foil and coat it with nonstick cooking spray. Arrange the skewers on the prepared baking sheet and roast them in the oven for 25 to 30 minutes, turning occasionally, until they are completely cooked. Check every 10 minutes to make sure they are not overcooked. Turn the broiler on for 5 minutes to give them a nice char.

3. Serve the kabobs warm with sumac or lemon juice and chelo or fresh warm bread.

BEEF & TOMATOES

—— واویشکا VAVISHKA ——

Serves 4
Prep: 10 minutes
Cook: 55 minutes

6 tablespoons vegetable
oil, divided

1 large yellow onion,
finely chopped

8 ounces beef stew meat,
cut into ½-inch cubes

¼ cup water

1 teaspoon ground turmeric

3 medium tomatoes, chopped
into small pieces

1 teaspoon salt

1 teaspoon freshly ground
black pepper

2 tablespoons tomato paste

1 large white potato, peeled
and cut into ½-inch cubes

MAKE IT EASIER **To
make this dish in less than
30 minutes, use ground
beef instead of stew meat.
Sauté the onion until it's
golden brown, add the
ground beef, and sauté
until the beef is browned.
Continue from step 3.**

WORTH THE WAIT To make Vavishka, one of the easiest Persian dishes from the north of Iran, you braise small pieces of beef in water, then fry them with tomatoes and spices. This makes the meat tender and savory. Vavishka can be served with bread, fried potatoes, or Kateh (page 22). Or, for an authentically Persian take on steak and eggs, try cracking an egg right into the pan in the last 10 minutes of cooking.

1. Heat 1 tablespoon of vegetable oil in a large pot over medium heat. When the oil begins to shimmer, add the onion and sauté until it's golden brown, about 10 minutes. Transfer the onion to a small plate and set it aside.

2. Add the beef and water to the same pot, cover, and cook for about 20 minutes, until there is no more water in the pot.

3. Add 2 tablespoons of vegetable oil to the pot, stir well, then add the turmeric, chopped tomatoes, and sautéed onion. Cook uncovered until the water released from the tomatoes has evaporated, 5 to 10 minutes. Add the salt, pepper, and tomato paste and mix everything together. Turn the heat to low and let the meat cook slowly as you fry the potatoes.

4. In a large nonstick skillet, heat the remaining 3 table-spoons of vegetable oil over medium heat. Add the potato, cook undisturbed for 5 minutes or until the cubes are browned on the bottom, then continue cooking, turning the potatoes every 3 to 5 minutes, until they are crispy and tender, about 10 minutes more.

5. Serve the meat hot with the fried potatoes and some rice or bread, if you'd like.

BEEF PATTIES

Serves 4
Prep: 25 minutes
Cook: 30 minutes

1 large white potato, peeled and cut into 8 pieces

1 large yellow onion

8 ounces lean ground beef

1 large egg

3 tablespoons all-purpose flour

1 teaspoon ground turmeric

1 teaspoon salt

4 to 6 tablespoons vegetable oil

Pita bread, rice, pickled vegetables, tomatoes, and fried potatoes, for serving

Kotlet is a very common Persian dish because it's easy to make and the ingredients—potatoes, onions, ground beef, and eggs—are available everywhere. It is usually fried in a skillet, but it can also be baked in the oven: Place the patties on a baking sheet lined with parchment paper, brush them lightly with vegetable oil, and bake them in a 375°F oven for 30 minutes, flipping them halfway through. The patties freeze really well and can be eaten in a wrap, with pita bread, or with plain white rice. They're typically served with a side of fried potatoes, pickled vegetables, and tomatoes.

1. Bring a large pot of water to a boil over high heat, add the potato pieces, and boil for 15 to 20 minutes, until fork tender. Drain and set aside to cool. When they are cool to the touch, transfer the potatoes to a large bowl and mash them with a potato masher.

2. Grate the onion. Squeeze the grated onion well in a clean kitchen towel or place it in a fine-mesh colander and press it with the back of a wooden spoon to extract as much liquid as possible. Discard the excess water.

3. In a large bowl, mix together the ground beef, grated onion, and mashed potatoes, using your hands. Add the egg, flour, turmeric, and salt. Mix until everything is well combined.

4. Heat the vegetable oil in a medium skillet over medium heat. Place a bowl of water nearby for your hands. Wet your hands with a little water, grab 1½ tablespoons of the meat mixture, and shape it into an oval patty.

5. Fry the patty in the vegetable oil for 3 to 4 minutes on each side until brown and crispy. Transfer the cooked patty to a paper towel–lined plate to drain, and repeat with the rest of the beef mixture, wetting your hands each time before you shape a patty, and adding more oil to the pan if needed.

6. Serve the warm patties with pita bread, rice, pickled vegetables, tomatoes, and fried potatoes.

COOKING TIP **Wetting your hands before shaping the patties will keep the beef mixture from getting too sticky.**

BEEF & SPLIT CHICKPEA PATTIES

—— شامی رشتی SHAMI RASHTI ——

Serves 4
Prep: 25 minutes,
plus 2 hours to soak
the beans
Cook: 2 hours, 30 minutes

1 pound beef stew meat,
cut into 1-inch cubes

1 large yellow onion,
cut into 6 pieces

1½ teaspoons ground
turmeric, divided

2 cups water

1 pound split chickpeas,
soaked in water for 2 hours

1 large white potato, peeled
and cut into 8 pieces

6 large eggs

3 tablespoons bloomed
saffron (see page 21)

1½ teaspoons salt

1 teaspoon freshly ground
black pepper

¼ to ½ cup vegetable oil

Pita bread, sliced tomatoes,
pickled cucumbers, and
fresh herbs, for serving

WORTH THE WAIT This is a more complicated version of Kotlet. This dish is usually made in the northern part of Iran, especially in the city of Rasht, which is why it's called Rashti. Shami Rashti is made from slow-cooked beef pieces mashed with potatoes and split chickpeas. The mixture freezes very well, so you can make a big batch. Put the meat mixture in smaller airtight containers after mashing everything but before adding the eggs. When you want to make the patties, let the mixture defrost and then continue from step 3.

1. In a large pot over medium heat, combine the beef, onion, 1 teaspoon of turmeric, and the water. Cover and cook for 1 hour, then add the split chickpeas and potato, and, if needed, ½ cup more water. Cook uncovered for 1 more hour, until the beef is very tender and the water is almost gone. Carefully pour out any remaining water.

2. Using a potato masher or immersion blender, mash or purée the beef, potatoes, and chickpeas so that they all stick together. Alternatively, transfer the mixture to a food processor and purée until smooth.

3. Place the mixture in a large bowl and add the eggs, saffron, salt, remaining ½ teaspoon of turmeric, and the pepper. Using your hands, knead and mix everything very well.

4. Heat the vegetable oil in a medium skillet over medium heat. Place a bowl of water nearby for your hands. Wet your hands with a little water and grab 1½ tablespoons of the meat mixture. Shape the mixture into a circle and make a small hole in the middle using your finger. Fry the patty for 4 to 5 minutes on each side, until both sides are brown. Transfer the cooked patty to a paper towel–lined plate to drain, and repeat with the rest of the beef mixture, wetting your hands each time before you shape a patty, and adding more oil to the pan if needed.

5. Serve the warm patties with pita bread, tomatoes, pickled cucumbers, and fresh herbs such as parsley and basil.

COOKING TIP This mixture might be a bit flimsy, and that's how it should be. If it's too difficult to work with, add just 1 tablespoon of all-purpose flour.

SUBSTITUTION TIP This dish is commonly made with lamb, so feel free to substitute the beef in this recipe with 1 pound of lamb.

MEATBALLS IN TOMATO SAUCE

سر گنجشکی SAR GONJESHKI

Serves 4
Prep: 20 minutes
Cook: 45 minutes

FOR THE MEATBALLS

1 small yellow onion

8 ounces lean ground beef

½ teaspoon ground cumin

½ teaspoon salt

½ teaspoon ground turmeric

½ teaspoon cayenne pepper

WORTH THE WAIT Sar Gonjeshki is simply meatballs cooked in tomato sauce with cubes of potatoes. It's very nutritious and is a full meal on its own. The name means "sparrow's head"; that's because the size of the meatballs should be as big as a sparrow's head, which is roughly 1 inch. Because these meatballs are small, they cook very quickly.

TO MAKE THE MEATBALLS

1. Grate the onion. Squeeze the grated onion well in a clean kitchen towel or place it in a fine-mesh colander and press it with the back of a wooden spoon to extract as much liquid as possible. Discard the excess water.

2. In a large bowl, mix the grated onion with the ground beef, cumin, salt, turmeric, and cayenne. Knead the mixture well with your hands until everything is completely combined.

3. Wet your hands and form the mixture into 1-inch-diameter meatballs. Set them aside.

FOR THE SAUCE

2 tablespoons vegetable oil

1 medium yellow onion, finely chopped

2 tablespoons tomato paste

½ teaspoon salt

½ teaspoon freshly ground black pepper

2 cups water

1 large white potato, peeled and cut into 1-inch chunks

Fresh bread and chopped fresh basil and parsley, for serving

Freshly squeezed lemon juice, for serving (optional)

TO MAKE THE SAUCE

1. Heat the vegetable oil in a large saucepan over medium heat. When the oil begins to shimmer, add the onion and sauté until it's golden brown, about 10 minutes. Stir in the tomato paste, salt, and pepper, and cook for 3 minutes. Add the water and stir until the tomato paste is completely dissolved. Cover the pan and bring the liquid to a boil.

2. When the sauce starts to boil, remove the lid and add the potato chunks and meatballs. Reduce the heat to low and simmer uncovered for 25 to 30 minutes, until the potatoes are tender and the meatballs are browned all the way through.

3. Serve the Sar Gonjeshki warm with some fresh bread and chopped herbs on the side. If you like, squeeze a little lemon juice over the dish when serving to give it a nice tanginess.

SUBSTITUTION TIP This dish can be made with ground chicken or turkey instead of ground beef.

BEEF & CARROT MEATBALLS

كوفته هويج KOOFTEH HAVIJ

Serves 6
Prep: 20 minutes
Cook: 50 minutes

FOR THE MEATBALLS

1 medium yellow onion

1 pound carrots, peeled

1 pound lean ground beef

1 large egg

2 tablespoons chickpea flour

1 teaspoon ground turmeric

1 teaspoon cayenne pepper

1 teaspoon salt

1 teaspoon freshly ground black pepper

3 tablespoons vegetable oil

WORTH THE WAIT Koofteh Havij is a meatball dish with a very unique flavor, mostly due to its balance of sweet carrot and spicy cayenne and black pepper. The meatballs are seared in vegetable oil and then cooked in a simple, thick sauce. Chickpea flour, also called gram flour, is available at Indian and Middle Eastern markets, and also in many health food stores.

TO MAKE THE MEATBALLS

1. Grate the onion and carrots separately. Squeeze them in separate, clean kitchen towels or place them separately in a fine-mesh colander and press them with the back of a wooden spoon to extract as much liquid as possible. Discard the excess water.

2. Place the grated onion and carrots in a large bowl. Add the ground beef, egg, chickpea flour, turmeric, cayenne, salt, and pepper. Knead the mixture with your hands until everything is well combined.

3. Wet your hands and shape the mixture into 1½-inch-diameter meatballs.

4. Heat the vegetable oil in a large skillet over medium heat. When the oil begins to shimmer, add the meatballs to the skillet and cook them until they are brown on all sides, 6 to 8 minutes total. Remove the skillet from the heat and set it aside.

FOR THE SAUCE

2 tablespoons vegetable oil

1 medium yellow onion, finely chopped

½ teaspoon ground turmeric

½ teaspoon cayenne pepper

2 tablespoons tomato paste

1½ cups water

TO MAKE THE SAUCE

1. Heat the vegetable oil in a large saucepan over medium-high heat. When the oil begins to shimmer, add the onion and sauté until it's golden brown, about 10 minutes. Add the turmeric, cayenne, and tomato paste. Stir and cook for 1 minute, then add the water. Stir well until the tomato paste is completely dissolved. Bring the sauce to a boil, then turn the heat to medium.

2. Place the meatballs in the sauce in a single layer and simmer for 30 minutes, spooning the sauce over the top every 10 minutes, until the meatballs are browned all the way through. Serve warm.

MAKE IT EASIER Preheat the oven to 375°F and roast the meatballs on a baking sheet for 20 minutes. Then place them in the sauce to cook.

BEEF & EGGPLANT MEATBALLS

کوفته بادمجان KOOFTEH BADEMJAAN

Serves 6
Prep: 30 minutes
Cook: 1 hour, 10 minutes

FOR THE MEATBALLS

6 Japanese eggplants, peeled and halved lengthwise

½ cup long-grain white rice, such as basmati, rinsed and drained

1 cup water

1 medium yellow onion

3 garlic cloves, minced

1 pound lean ground beef

½ cup finely chopped walnuts

1 teaspoon ground turmeric

1 teaspoon salt

1 teaspoon freshly ground black pepper

1 cup breadcrumbs

3 tablespoons vegetable oil

WORTH THE WAIT These tender meatballs get their earthy, almost sweet flavor and satisfying texture from tender eggplant and crunchy walnuts. In this recipe, I roast the eggplants, but if you want to add a tinge of smokiness, feel free to grill them instead. The meatballs are browned in oil and then simmered in a little tomato sauce and served with fresh bread. Make sure the sauce is simmering when you add the meatballs to it; otherwise the meatballs may break.

TO MAKE THE MEATBALLS

1. Preheat the oven to 375°F. Place the eggplants on a rimmed baking sheet and roast them in the oven for about 20 minutes, until they are very tender. Remove the baking sheet from the oven and let the eggplants cool slightly, then transfer them to a food processor or blender and purée until smooth.

2. While the eggplants are roasting, combine the rice and water in a small saucepan over medium heat. Bring the water to a boil, then cover the pan and simmer for 15 to 20 minutes or until all the water has been absorbed. Remove the pan from the heat and set it aside.

3. Grate the onion. Squeeze it well in a clean kitchen towel or place it in a fine-mesh colander and press it with the back of a wooden spoon to extract as much liquid as possible. Discard the excess water.

4. Combine the puréed eggplant, cooked rice, grated onion, garlic, ground beef, walnuts, turmeric, salt, and pepper in a large bowl. Mix with your hands until everything is fully incorporated.

FOR THE SAUCE

2 tablespoons vegetable oil

1 medium yellow onion, finely chopped

½ teaspoon ground turmeric

½ teaspoon salt

2 tablespoons tomato paste

2 cups water

5. Place the breadcrumbs on a flat plate. Line a large baking sheet with parchment paper. Wet your hands and form the meat mixture into 1-inch-diameter meatballs. Roll the meatballs in the breadcrumbs and place them on the prepared baking sheet.

6. Heat the vegetable oil in a large skillet over medium heat. When the oil begins to shimmer, add the meatballs to the skillet and cook them until they are brown on all sides, 6 to 8 minutes total. Remove the skillet from the heat and set it aside.

TO MAKE THE SAUCE

1. Heat the vegetable oil in a large saucepan over medium-high heat. When the oil begins to shimmer, add the onion and sauté until it's golden brown, about 10 minutes. Add the turmeric, salt, and tomato paste. Stir and cook for 1 minute, then add the water. Stir until the tomato paste is completely dissolved. Bring the sauce to a boil, then turn the heat to medium.

2. Place the meatballs in the sauce in a single layer and simmer for 30 minutes, spooning the sauce over the top every 10 minutes, until the meatballs are browned all the way through. Serve warm.

MAKE IT EASIER Rather than cooking a whole new batch of rice, use 1 cup of leftover cooked rice.

BEEF & MINT MEATBALLS

کوفته نخودچی KOOFTEH NOKHODCHI

Serves 4
Prep: 20 minutes
Cook: 1 hour

FOR THE MEATBALLS

1 medium yellow onion

1 pound lean ground beef

3 tablespoons chickpea flour

1 teaspoon salt

1 tablespoon dried mint

1 teaspoon freshly ground
black pepper

WORTH THE WAIT Koofteh Nokhodchi (also called
Ghermezeh Nokhodchi) is a meatball dish from the
central Iranian city of Isfahan, in which mint and
chickpea flour are star ingredients. Because the
meatballs are not seared before they are added to
the sauce, they are delicate and may fall apart if the
sauce isn't hot enough. If the sauce stops simmering
while adding the meatballs, bring it to a simmer
again and then continue adding the meatballs.

TO MAKE THE MEATBALLS

1. Grate the onion. Squeeze it well in a clean kitchen towel
or place it in a fine-mesh colander and press it with the back of
a wooden spoon to extract as much liquid as possible. Discard
the excess water.

2. In a large bowl, combine the grated onion, ground beef,
chickpea flour, salt, dried mint, and pepper. Knead the mixture
with your hands until all the ingredients are well incorporated.

3. Wet your hands and form the mixture into 2½-inch-
diameter meatballs. Set them aside.

FOR THE SAUCE

2 tablespoons vegetable oil

1 medium yellow onion, finely chopped

½ teaspoon ground turmeric

2 tablespoons tomato paste

1½ cups water

1 tablespoon dried mint

TO MAKE THE SAUCE

1. Heat the vegetable oil in a large pan over medium-high heat. When the oil begins to shimmer, add the onion and sauté until it's golden brown, about 10 minutes. Add the turmeric and tomato paste. Stir and cook for 1 minute, then add the water and dried mint. Stir until the tomato paste is completely dissolved. Bring the sauce to a boil, then turn the heat to medium. The sauce should be bubbling gently.

2. Place the meatballs in the simmering sauce in a single layer and cook for 40 to 50 minutes, spooning the sauce over the top every 10 minutes, until the meatballs are browned all the way through. Serve warm.

MAKE IT EASIER Instead of kneading the beef mixture with your hands, transfer the ingredients to a food processor and pulse until everything is evenly incorporated.

POMEGRANATE & WALNUT MEATBALLS

کوفته انار و گردو KOOFTEH ANAR-O-GERDOO

Serves 4
Prep: 15 minutes
Cook: 50 minutes

FOR THE MEATBALLS

1 medium yellow onion

8 ounces lean ground beef

8 ounces ground lamb

1 cup finely chopped walnuts

⅓ cup finely chopped fresh parsley

1 large egg

¼ cup breadcrumbs

1 teaspoon salt

½ teaspoon ground turmeric

½ teaspoon cayenne pepper

3 tablespoons vegetable oil

WORTH THE WAIT The distinctive flavors of Persian cuisine are combined in Koofteh Anar-o-Gerdoo, a delicious dish made of ground lamb and beef, pomegranate molasses, walnuts, and spices. You can make a large batch of these meatballs in advance, freeze them after you sear them, then thaw them in the refrigerator overnight and cook them in the sauce for 30 minutes.

TO MAKE THE MEATBALLS

1. Grate the onion. Squeeze it well in a clean kitchen towel or place it in a fine-mesh colander and press it with the back of a wooden spoon to extract as much liquid as possible. Discard the excess water.

2. In a large bowl, combine the beef, lamb, walnuts, and parsley. Knead the mixture with your hands until everything is well combined. Crack the egg into the bowl, then add the breadcrumbs, salt, turmeric, and cayenne. Knead well.

3. Wet your hands and form the mixture into 1½-inch-diameter meatballs.

4. Heat the vegetable oil in a large skillet over medium heat. When the oil begins to shimmer, add the meatballs to the skillet and cook them until they are brown on all sides, 6 to 8 minutes total. Remove the skillet from the heat and set it aside.

FOR THE SAUCE

2 tablespoons vegetable oil

1 medium yellow onion, finely sliced

½ cup pomegranate molasses

1 tablespoon sugar (optional)

½ cup water

TO MAKE THE SAUCE

1. Heat the vegetable oil in a large saucepan over medium-high heat. When the oil begins to shimmer, add the onion and sauté until it's caramelized and golden, about 10 minutes.

2. Add the pomegranate molasses and sugar (if using), then pour in the water. Bring the liquid to a boil and reduce the heat to medium.

3. Place the meatballs in the simmering sauce in a single layer and cook for 20 to 30 minutes, spooning the sauce over the top every 10 minutes, until the meatballs are browned all the way through. Serve warm.

MAKE IT EASIER Preheat the oven to 375°F and roast the meatballs on a baking sheet for 20 minutes. Then place them in the sauce to cook.

TABRIZI MEATBALLS

كوفته تبريزى KOOFTEH TABRIZI

Serves 6
Prep: 30 minutes
Cook: 1 hour, 30 minutes

FOR THE STUFFING

2 tablespoons vegetable oil, divided

1 medium yellow onion, finely chopped

⅓ cup chopped walnuts

⅓ cup barberries, rinsed and dried

8 whole Persian dried plums

½ teaspoon salt

½ teaspoon ground turmeric

WORTH THE WAIT These jumbo-size meatballs are about 4 inches in diameter and stuffed with barberries, fried onions, walnuts, and Persian dried plums. Some people stuff them with peeled hard-boiled eggs as well, which results in even bigger meatballs. The meatballs are cooked in tomato sauce, then transferred to small individual plates for serving; the sauce is spooned into one big bowl and passed at the table along with a plate of lavash. It's a bit of work to make Koofteh Tabrizi, so I recommend tackling it on a weekend day when you have plenty of time.

TO MAKE THE STUFFING

1. Heat the vegetable oil in a large skillet over medium heat. When the oil begins to shimmer, add the onion and sauté until it's caramelized and golden, about 10 minutes.

2. Add the walnuts, barberries, and Persian dried plums to the skillet. Stir for 1 minute, then mix in the salt and turmeric. Turn off the heat and set the skillet aside.

FOR THE MEATBALLS

½ cup dried split chickpeas, rinsed and drained

½ cup long-grain white rice, such as basmati, rinsed and drained

1½ cups water

1 medium yellow onion

1 pound lean ground beef

2 large eggs

1 teaspoon salt

1 teaspoon freshly ground black pepper

½ teaspoon ground cinnamon

½ teaspoon ground turmeric

2 tablespoons chopped fresh tarragon

2 tablespoons chopped fresh cilantro

TO MAKE THE MEATBALLS

1. Place the split chickpeas and rice in a medium saucepan and add the water. Place the pan over medium heat, bring the water to a boil, and cook for 10 minutes, until the split chickpeas are almost soft. Drain the rice and chickpeas and transfer them to a food processor or a blender; purée until smooth. Set aside.

2. Grate the onion. Squeeze it well in a clean kitchen towel or place it in a fine-mesh colander and press it with the back of a wooden spoon to extract as much liquid as possible. Discard the excess water.

3. In a large bowl, combine the chickpea and rice mixture, grated onion, and ground beef. Knead the mixture with your hands until everything is very well combined. Add the eggs, salt, pepper, cinnamon, turmeric, tarragon, and cilantro. Keep kneading until everything is thoroughly combined and you have a sticky mixture.

4. Divide the mixture into six equal portions. Wet your hands and shape one portion into a ball. Hold it in the palm of your hand and make a depression in the center with your fingers. Spoon one sixth of the stuffing into the depression, then bring the beef mixture around the stuffing and shape it into a ball. Repeat with the remaining meat mixture and stuffing. Set all the giant meatballs aside.

FOR THE SAUCE

2 tablespoons vegetable oil

1 medium yellow onion, finely chopped

2 tablespoons tomato paste

1 teaspoon salt

1 teaspoon freshly ground black pepper

2 cups water

Dry thin crispy bread, preferably lavash, for serving

TO MAKE THE SAUCE

1. Heat the vegetable oil in a large pot over medium heat. When the oil begins to shimmer, add the onion and sauté until it's golden brown, about 10 minutes. Add the tomato paste and sauté for 1 minute, then stir in the salt and pepper. Pour in the water and stir until the tomato paste is completely dissolved.

2. Turn the heat up to medium high and bring the sauce to a boil, then turn the heat down to medium low and let the sauce simmer for 5 minutes.

3. Place all the meatballs very carefully in the sauce. The sauce should come about halfway up the meatballs. Do not cover the pot (the meatballs will fall apart!) and do not move the meatballs for the first 30 minutes of cooking. After 30 minutes, carefully turn the meatballs and add more water if the sauce is too thick. Cook for an additional 20 minutes, carefully spooning the sauce over the meatballs every 5 minutes or so.

4. Serve the meatballs and sauce separately, along with lavash or other dried thin bread.

INGREDIENT TIP **Use half ground beef and half ground lamb for the meatballs; they'll have a richer flavor and stick together better.**

LAMB LIVER & POTATOES

جغور بغور — JAGHOOR BAGHOOR

Serves 4
Prep: 10 minutes
Cook: 50 minutes

7 tablespoons vegetable oil, divided

2 large yellow onions, thinly sliced

1 pound lamb's liver, cut into 1-inch cubes

1½ teaspoons ground turmeric

1 teaspoon salt

1 teaspoon freshly ground black pepper

2 tablespoons tomato paste

¼ cup water

1 large white potato, peeled and cut into ½-inch cubes

Fresh warm bread, for serving

WORTH THE WAIT Jaghoor Baghoor is a kind of Persian fast food dish starring lamb's liver, but some people also use the heart, lungs, and kidneys. (Calf's liver is tougher and has a different flavor, so it is not a good substitute.) In this dish, lots of onion, turmeric, and starchy potato balance the earthy, mineral taste of the liver.

1. Heat 3 tablespoons of vegetable oil in a large skillet over medium heat. When the oil begins to shimmer, add the onions and sauté until they are golden brown, about 10 minutes. Then add the liver and sauté until the pieces are light brown on all sides, about 5 minutes. Add the turmeric, salt, and pepper to the skillet. Stir well until the spices coat all the liver pieces.

2. Add the tomato paste to the skillet and stir for 1 minute. Add the water, cover the skillet, and cook for 20 to 30 minutes, until the liver is cooked through. Remove the lid and continue cooking until all the water has evaporated, 3 to 5 minutes longer.

3. While the liver is cooking, heat the remaining 4 tablespoons of vegetable oil in a large skillet. When the oil begins to shimmer, add the potato cubes and fry them for 10 to 15 minutes or until crispy and tender. Remove the skillet from the heat and set it aside.

4. When the liver is cooked and the pan is dry, add the fried potatoes and stir well until everything is incorporated.

5. Serve hot with fresh warm bread.

COOKING TIP Make sure there is no water left in the pan before adding the fried potatoes. Water might make the potatoes slimy, and in this dish they should stay crispy.

WINTER LAMB & POTATOES

تاس کباب TAAS KABOB

Serves 4
Prep: 15 minutes
Cook: 1 hour

2 large yellow onions

2 quinces, peeled

4 tablespoons vegetable oil, divided

8 ounces lamb loin, cut into 1-inch cubes

½ cup Persian dried plums, divided

2 teaspoons salt, divided

2 teaspoons freshly ground black pepper, divided

1 cup water, divided

2 medium white potatoes, peeled

1 tablespoon tomato paste

Fresh lemon wedges, for serving

WORTH THE WAIT Taas Kabob is a very simple Persian dish that has been made by Iranians for years. It's made from layers of vegetables and lamb that are cooked in just a little bit of water. This dish may take more or less time to cook, depending on the meat. (For a vegan option, simply leave out the lamb and add some mushrooms instead.) It includes quince, which grows on small trees and is closely related to apples and pears. This fruit is not tasty in its raw state, but when cooked it has a delicious, floral flavor and a delicate fragrance of vanilla, citrus, and apple. Since quince is available in fall and winter, Taas Kabob is considered a winter dish.

1. Slice the onions into thin rounds and set them aside. Core the quinces and cut each one into 12 wedges.

2. Pour 2 tablespoons of vegetable oil into the bottom of a large pot. Spread one third of the onions across the bottom of the pot, then top them with half of the lamb pieces, ¼ cup of Persian dried plums, and one third of the quince wedges. Sprinkle 1 teaspoon of salt and 1 teaspoon of black pepper on top. Repeat the layers twice more (no lamb for the last layer). Pour the remaining 2 tablespoons of vegetable oil on top of the last layer. Carefully pour ½ cup of water into the pot, being careful not to disturb the layers.

3. Cover the pot, place it over medium heat, and cook for 40 minutes, until the lamb is completely browned and tender.

4. Slice the potatoes into thin rounds and layer them on top in the pot. In a small bowl, whisk the tomato paste into the remaining ½ cup of water and carefully pour this mixture over the potatoes in the pot. Cover the pot and cook for another 20 minutes or until the potatoes are very tender. Remove the pot from the heat.

5. Using a flat spatula, cut the Taas Kabob into wedges, like a cake. Serve the wedges in individual plates or bowls with the lemon wedges for squeezing.

MAKE IT EASIER You can layer everything—including the potatoes and tomato paste mixture—in a slow cooker and cook the Taas Kabob on low for 8 hours.

MAMANI'S FISH

ماهی مامانی MAHI MAMANI

Serves 4
Prep: 10 minutes
Cook: 45 minutes

2 tablespoons vegetable oil

1 pound mahi mahi fillets

2 medium white potatoes, peeled and cut into ½-inch-thick slices

1 teaspoon ground turmeric

1½ teaspoons salt, divided

¼ cup water

6 garlic cloves, peeled

1 teaspoon ground cinnamon

Chelo (page 104) or Herbs & Rice (page 106), for serving

INGREDIENT TIP Fresh fillets work best for this recipe. However, if you're using frozen mahi mahi, defrost it completely before starting the recipe. Also, the fillets must be completely dry before frying.

This is the way my maman's maman (my grandmother) used to make fish. She would brown the fillets in a large skillet, then cook up some potatoes in the same pan, season them with turmeric, garlic, and cinnamon, put the browned fish on top, and continue cooking until it flaked easily with a fork. The garlic gives this dish a very nice flavor.

1. Heat the vegetable oil in a large skillet over medium heat. When the oil begins to shimmer, carefully place the mahi mahi fillets in the skillet in one layer and fry them until they are browned on the bottom, 6 to 8 minutes. Turn the fillets over and fry the other side until brown, then transfer the fish to a plate and set it aside.

2. Place the potatoes in one layer at the bottom of the same skillet. Sprinkle the potatoes with the turmeric and 1 teaspoon of salt. Add the water, cover the skillet, and cook for 10 minutes, until the potatoes are half cooked.

3. Place the fish fillets on top of the potatoes and tuck the garlic cloves between the fillets. Sprinkle with the remaining ½ teaspoon of salt and the cinnamon. Cook for 20 minutes more, until the potatoes are completely tender and the flavors have blended.

4. Serve warm with chelo or Herbs & Rice.

My Memories

In my family, fish is served for many different occasions, such as the longest night of the year (Yalda), the last Wednesday of the year (Chaharshanbe Soori), and the last night of the year. Sometimes we make my grandmother's recipe (page 142), and sometimes we make Stuffed Fish (page 144), which is another old family recipe. My grandmother's recipe is more on the mildly sweet side because of the turmeric and cinnamon, whereas in the other recipe, the fish has more of a sour and tangy taste because of the barberries and

pomegranate molasses. We like to serve the fish with Herbs & Rice (page 106) or sometimes Chelo (page 104).

The days before and after the New Year always evoke a lot of memories for me. Those are the days when everyone is busy: They are doing the spring cleaning, buying new clothes, and some are baking Norooz cookies or planning to go on a vacation for Norooz holiday. The weather gets nicer and you can see new leaves on the trees. Shops sell colorful flowers, which are used as decorations for the Haft-Seen, a set of seven symbolic items traditionally displayed on the table during Norooz.

Those days are all about happiness, kindness, and sharing. One year, my friends and I visited a children's cancer treatment center and an orphanage and put on an entertaining show for them. We sang songs, painted, and played games. It was such a rewarding experience for me, because I learned that your New Year is even happier when you help others find happiness too.

STUFFED FISH

ماهی شکم پر MAHI SHEKAM POR

Serves 4
Prep: 20 minutes,
plus 30 minutes
for marinating
Cook: 30 minutes

FOR THE FISH

4 small whole trout,
cleaned and gutted

1 medium yellow
onion, grated

4 garlic cloves, minced

1 teaspoon ground turmeric

1 teaspoon salt

1 teaspoon freshly ground
black pepper

3 tablespoons olive oil

2 tablespoons freshly
squeezed lemon juice

WORTH THE WAIT Mahi Shekam Por is a really different way to serve fish. The star of the dish is definitely the stuffing, which has a slightly sour taste because of the barberries and pomegranate molasses. The recipe here calls for small trout, but you can use any other small whole fish. This recipe also works well with big, meaty fillets, such as salmon—just pile the stuffing on top.

TO MAKE THE FISH

1. Pat the fish dry with paper towels, making sure the inside is very clean.

2. In a large bowl, mix together the grated onion, garlic, turmeric, salt, pepper, olive oil, and lemon juice to form a paste. Rub the paste on both sides of and inside each fish. Place the fish in a baking dish, cover with plastic wrap, and refrigerate for 30 minutes.

3. Preheat the oven to 400°F. Line a baking sheet with two layers of parchment paper.

4. Place the marinated fish on the prepared baking sheet. Roast the fish for 30 minutes, until it is easily flaked with a fork. Make the stuffing while the fish cooks.

FOR THE STUFFING

1 tablespoon olive oil

1 medium yellow onion, finely chopped

2 garlic cloves, minced

1 bell pepper (any color), seeded and diced

1 teaspoon salt

1 teaspoon freshly ground black pepper

1 teaspoon ground turmeric

2 teaspoons dried rosemary or 1 tablespoon chopped fresh

2 teaspoons dried thyme or 1 tablespoon chopped fresh

¾ cup chopped walnuts

½ cup barberries, rinsed and dried

3 tablespoons pomegranate molasses

FOR SERVING

Fresh lemon wedges

TO MAKE THE STUFFING

While the fish cooks, heat the olive oil in a large skillet over medium heat. When the oil begins to shimmer, add the onion and garlic and sauté until the onion is golden brown, about 10 minutes. Add the bell pepper, sauté for 2 minutes more, then stir in the salt, pepper, turmeric, rosemary, thyme, and walnuts. Cook for 3 minutes more, stir in the barberries, and add the pomegranate molasses. Mix well until everything is well combined. Remove the skillet from the heat.

TO SERVE

Spoon some stuffing into the cavity of each fish and top with any remaining stuffing. Serve the fish warm with freshly squeezed lemon juice.

SUBSTITUTION TIP To make this dish with a salmon fillet, preheat the oven to 400°F, rub the salmon with a little olive oil, and bake it for 25 minutes. Then mound the stuffing on top and serve.

7 MIXED RICE DISHES

ONE-POT RICE & TOMATOES

دمی گوجه فرنگی DAMI GOJEH FARANGI

Serves 4
Prep: 10 minutes
Cook: 35 minutes

2 tablespoons vegetable oil

1 medium yellow onion,
finely chopped

½ teaspoon ground turmeric

2 medium white
potatoes, diced

5 large canned or fresh
tomatoes, peeled and crushed
(see Cooking Tip)

1 teaspoon salt

½ teaspoon cayenne pepper

2 cups long-grain white rice,
such as basmati, rinsed
and drained

2 to 3 cups water

Yogurt and chopped fresh
herbs, for serving

VEGAN Dami Gojeh Farangi is a one-pot Persian dish that is made from crushed tomatoes, onions, potatoes, and rice. It has a denser texture than steamed white rice and pairs well with yogurt and fresh herbs such as parsley and mint.

1. Heat the vegetable oil in a large pot over medium heat. When the oil begins to shimmer, add the onion and sauté until it's golden brown, about 10 minutes. Stir in the turmeric, then add the potatoes and cook for 5 minutes.

2. Add the crushed tomatoes, salt, cayenne, rice, and 2 cups of water to the pot. Bring the liquid to a boil, turn the heat to low, and let it simmer until the water has almost completely evaporated, about 20 minutes. Take out a rice grain and check if it's cooked. If the grain is still hard, add ½ cup of water and let it simmer until the rice is tender. Wrap the lid in a clean towel and put it on the pot. Let the rice steam over medium-low heat for 10 minutes or until it is fully cooked.

3. Serve warm with yogurt and fresh herbs.

COOKING TIP To crush fresh tomatoes, cut an X at the bottom of each tomato and let them sit in hot water for 10 minutes to make the skin easier to remove. Peel them, transfer them to a food processor, and pulse until they are broken down.

SAVORY SAFFRON RICE CAKE

ته چین — TAHCHIN —

Serves 4
Prep: 10 minutes
Cook: 1 hour, 10 minutes

6¼ cups water, divided

2 cups long-grain white rice, such as basmati, rinsed and drained

2½ teaspoons salt, divided

Nonstick cooking spray

1 cup plain Greek yogurt

3 large eggs

½ cup vegetable oil

1 teaspoon salt

4 tablespoons bloomed saffron (see page 21)

Sautéed barberries, slivered almonds, and pistachios, for topping (optional)

WHY IT WORKS Tahchin was originally cooked in a pot on the stove, but because you couldn't see the bottom, it often ended up burning. This recipe ensures a great tahchin that has been cooked evenly to perfection.

VEGETARIAN, WORTH THE WAIT Tahchin is a dense and delicious Persian rice dish that is flavored with yogurt and saffron and can be cut into pieces for serving. It's typically served with Chicken with Tomato Sauce (page 98).

1. Pour 6 cups of water into a large nonstick pot and bring it to a boil over high heat. Add the rinsed rice and 1½ teaspoons of salt. Let the rice boil for about 10 minutes. Check one grain by pressing it between your thumb and index finger; you should be able to break the grain but it should still be hard in the center. Remove the pot from the heat.

2. Preheat the oven to 350°F. Coat an 8-by 8-inch glass baking dish with nonstick cooking spray.

3. Place a colander in the sink and drain the rice. In a large bowl, mix the rice, yogurt, eggs, vegetable oil, salt, and bloomed saffron. Pour the mixture into the prepared baking dish, cover with aluminum foil, and, using a sharp knife, make four to six holes in the aluminum foil so the steam can escape. Bake the rice in the oven for 1 hour or until it is firm and the bottom is golden brown.

4. Remove the rice cake from the oven and let it cool for 5 minutes. Place a plate on top of the pan and flip the tahchin into the plate.

5. Serve warm, topped with sautéed barberries, slivered almonds, and pistachios (if using).

RICE WITH MUNG BEANS

ماش پلو MAASH POLO

Serves 4
Prep: 10 minutes,
plus 2 hours to soak
the beans
Cook: 1 hour, 20 minutes

1 cup dried mung beans,
soaked in water for 2 hours
and drained

8⅓ cups water, divided

8 tablespoons vegetable
oil, divided

2 medium yellow onions,
finely chopped

1 teaspoon ground turmeric

2 cups long-grain white rice,
such as basmati, rinsed
and drained

1½ teaspoons salt

Thin bread for the bottom of
the pot (lavash works best)

½ teaspoon ground cinnamon

2 tablespoons bloomed
saffron (see page 21)

VEGAN, WORTH THE WAIT You'll find mung beans at Asian and Middle Eastern markets, and sometimes even in your local big-name grocery store. They are very nutritious, so this dish is usually served on its own with just a salad, though it is also delicious with Saffron Chicken (page 100). Maash Polo contains a lot of fried onion, which gives it a great texture and earthy-sweet flavor.

1. In a medium saucepan, combine the mung beans and 2 cups of water. Bring the water to a boil over high heat and cook for 30 to 40 minutes or until the beans are almost completely tender. Drain the beans and set them aside.

2. While the beans are boiling, heat 2 tablespoons of vegetable oil in a large skillet over medium heat. When the oil begins to shimmer, add the onions and sauté them until they're golden brown, about 10 minutes. Add the turmeric and stir for 2 minutes. Turn the heat off and set the onions aside.

3. Pour 6 cups of water into a large nonstick pot and bring it to a boil over high heat. Add the rice and salt and let it boil for almost 10 minutes. Check one grain by pressing it between your thumb and index finger; you should be able to break the grain but it should still be firm. Add the drained mung beans to the rice and let them boil for 30 seconds.

4. Place a colander in the sink and drain the rice and beans. Place the pot back over medium heat. Make sure the bottom of the pot is dry. Add 3 tablespoons of vegetable oil to the pot and place the bread in the pot so it covers the bottom entirely.

5. Scoop one third of the rice and beans into the pot and spread it in an even layer. Sprinkle with some of the cinnamon, then layer one third of the onions over the rice. Repeat with the remaining rice, cinnamon, and onions.

6. Carefully pour the remaining ⅓ cup of water around the edges of the pot. Wrap the lid in a clean towel and put it on the pot. Let the rice cook for 20 minutes, until the steam starts to escape. Pour the remaining 3 tablespoons of vegetable oil over the rice, cover, and steam for 10 minutes more.

7. Spoon out 1 cup of rice and mix it with the bloomed saffron. Serve the warm Maash Polo on a large platter topped with the saffron rice.

BEYOND THE BASICS For a meat dish, add 8 ounces lean ground beef to the sautéed onion and cook until the meat is completely brown, then add the turmeric and ½ teaspoon salt. Continue following the recipe.

CARROT MIXED RICE

هویج پلو HAVIJ POLO

Serves 4
Prep: 15 minutes
Cook: 1 hour

FOR THE FILLING

4 large carrots

2 tablespoons vegetable oil

1 medium yellow onion,
finely chopped

½ teaspoon ground turmeric

½ teaspoon salt

½ teaspoon freshly ground
black pepper

2 tablespoons bloomed
saffron (see page 21)

½ teaspoon ground cinnamon

VEGAN, WORTH THE WAIT Carrots and cinnamon give
Havij Polo a sweeter flavor than most other Polos and
make it an especially delicious accompaniment for
Saffron Chicken (page 100) or any meatball recipe
(pages 126 to 136).

TO MAKE THE FILLING

1. Peel the carrots and shred them using the largest holes
on your box grater. Set them aside.

2. Heat the vegetable oil in a large skillet over medium heat.
When the oil begins to shimmer, add the onion and sauté until
it's golden brown, about 10 minutes. Add the shredded carrot
and sauté for 5 to 10 minutes, until the carrot is tender and
bright orange. Add the turmeric, salt, pepper, saffron, and
cinnamon. Stir well and cook for 2 minutes more. Remove
the skillet from the heat and set it aside to cool.

FOR THE RICE

6⅓ cups water, divided

2 cups long-grain white rice, such as basmati, rinsed and drained

1½ teaspoons salt

6 tablespoons vegetable oil, divided

2 medium white potatoes, thinly sliced

TO MAKE THE RICE

1. Pour 6 cups of water into a large nonstick pot and bring it to a boil over high heat. Add the rice and salt and boil the rice for about 10 minutes. Check one grain by pressing it between your thumb and index finger; you should be able to break the grain but it should still be firm.

2. Place a colander in the sink and drain the rice. Place the pot back on the stove over medium heat. Make sure the bottom of the pot is dry. Add 3 tablespoons of vegetable oil and place the potato slices in the pot so they cover the bottom entirely.

3. Scoop one third of the rice back into the pot and layer half of the carrot and onion mixture on top. Repeat with the remaining rice and filling, finishing with a layer of rice. Carefully pour the remaining ⅓ cup of water around the edges of the pot. Wrap the lid in a clean towel and put it on the pot. Let the rice cook for 20 minutes, until the steam starts to escape from the bottom of the pot. Pour 3 tablespoons of vegetable oil over the rice, cover, and steam for 10 minutes more. Serve warm.

BEYOND THE BASICS To give Havij Polo a nice little tartness, add ½ cup barberries along with the carrots.

SOUR CHERRY MIXED RICE

 آلبالو پلو — ALBALOO POLO

Serves 4
Prep: 30 minutes
Cook: 1 hour, 10 minutes

6 ounces fresh sour
cherries, pitted

½ cup sugar

6¼ cups water, divided

2 cups long-grain white rice,
such as basmati, rinsed
and drained

1½ teaspoons salt

6 tablespoons vegetable
oil, divided

2 tablespoons bloomed
saffron (see page 21)

VEGAN, WORTH THE WAIT Albaloo Polo has a sweet
and sour taste and a lovely texture, all thanks to
the juicy sour cherries. These cherries (sometimes
called pie cherries) are smaller than their large, sweet
cousins, with a puckery flavor, as their name suggests.
To balance them out, here they are cooked with a
little sugar and then steamed with rice. This dish can
be served on its own, but it also pairs well with any
chicken recipe.

1. Combine the sour cherries and sugar in a small saucepan
over medium heat and cook until the cherries are soft and have
released some juice, about 15 minutes. Place a colander over
another saucepan and strain the cherries. Set the fruit aside.

2. Bring the cherry juice to a boil over medium heat, then
reduce the heat to medium low and simmer until the juice
thickens a little bit, about 5 minutes. Remove the pan from
the heat and set it aside.

3. Pour 6 cups of water into a large nonstick pot and bring
it to a boil over high heat. Add the rice and salt and boil for
about 10 minutes. Check one grain by pressing it between your
thumb and index finger; you should be able to break the grain
but it should still be firm.

4. Place a colander in the sink and drain the rice. Put the pot back on the stove over medium heat. Make sure the bottom of the pot is dry. Add 4 tablespoons of vegetable oil and the remaining ¼ cup of water to the pot and reduce the heat to medium low. In a small bowl, mix 5 tablespoons of rice with the bloomed saffron, then scoop it into the pot and spread it out so it covers the bottom entirely.

5. Scoop one third of the plain rice back into the pot, cover it with half of the sour cherries, add another one third of the rice, cover with the remaining cherries, and finish with the rest of the rice. Using the edge of a spatula, make 5 holes in the surface of the rice to let the steam escape.

6. Wrap the lid in a clean towel and put it on the pot. Let the rice cook for 20 minutes, until the steam starts to escape. Mix the remaining 2 tablespoons of vegetable oil with the sour cherry syrup and pour it over the rice. Cover to steam the rice for another 20 minutes, until the rice is completely tender. Serve warm.

INGREDIENT TIP Fresh sour cherries have a very short season in the early summer. Look for them in Middle Eastern grocery stores. If you can't find fresh sour cherries, use ¾ cup dried sour cherries instead. Just soak the dried cherries in water for 30 minutes, drain them well, and follow the recipe as written.

TUNA & POTATO MIXED RICE

تن ماهی و سیب زمینی TONEH MAHI VA SIBZAMINI

Serves 4
Prep: 15 minutes
Cook: 1 hour, 20 minutes

FOR THE FILLING

5 tablespoons vegetable oil, divided

2 large white potatoes, cut into ½-inch cubes

1 medium yellow onion, finely chopped

2 (6-ounce) cans tunafish packed in water, drained

1 teaspoon ground turmeric

½ teaspoon salt

½ teaspoon freshly ground black pepper

WORTH THE WAIT Toneh Mahi va Sibzamini is a dish my maman used to whip up when she wanted to make something delicious, healthy, and relatively quick. Unlike many Persian dishes, there's no saffron here; more turmeric is added to the filling instead. The rice is cooked separately and then served with tuna and potatoes. A few drops of lemon juice will make the dish taste even better.

TO MAKE THE FILLING

1. Heat 3 tablespoons of vegetable oil in a large skillet over medium heat. When the oil begins to shimmer, add the potato and sauté until it is golden brown and tender, 10 to 15 minutes. Transfer to a bowl and set aside.

2. In the same skillet, heat the remaining 2 tablespoons of vegetable oil over medium heat and sauté the onion until it's golden brown, about 10 minutes. Add the tuna and break it into small pieces using a spatula. Sauté for 3 to 5 minutes, until it's warm. Add the cooked potatoes, toss well, and season with the turmeric, salt, and pepper. Remove the skillet from the heat and set it aside.

FOR THE RICE

6½ cups water, divided

2 cups long-grain white rice, such as basmati, rinsed and drained

1½ teaspoons salt

6 tablespoons vegetable oil, divided

1 tablespoon bloomed saffron (see page 21)

Thin bread for the bottom of the pot (lavash works best)

TO MAKE THE RICE

1. Pour 6 cups of water into a large nonstick pot and bring it to a boil over high heat. Add the rice and salt and boil for about 10 minutes. Check one grain of rice by pressing it between your thumb and index finger; you should be able to break the grain but it should still be firm.

2. Place a colander in the sink and drain the rice. Place the pot back on the stove over medium heat. Make sure the bottom of the pot is dry. Heat 3 tablespoons of vegetable oil in the pot, add the bloomed saffron, and arrange the bread so it covers the bottom entirely.

3. Scoop the rice into the pot and use a spatula to push most of it to the middle, forming a mound. Carefully pour the remaining ½ cup of water around the edges of the pot. Using the edge of a spatula, make 5 holes in the surface of the rice to let the steam escape. Wrap the lid in a clean towel and put it on the pot. Let the rice cook for 30 minutes, until the steam starts to escape. Pour the remaining 3 tablespoons of vegetable oil over the rice, cover, and steam for 10 minutes more or until the rice is completely tender.

4. To serve, spread one third of the rice on a large platter and top with half of the tuna and potato mixture. Top with another third of the rice and the remaining tuna and potatoes. Finish with a final layer of rice.

MAKE IT EASIER Make Kateh (page 22) instead of chelo to save time. Make the filling as the rice is cooking to have this dish ready in 30 minutes.

SPICY SHRIMP MIXED RICE

 MEYGOO POLO

Serves 4
Prep: 20 minutes
Cook: 1 hour, 10 minutes

FOR THE FILLING

3 tablespoons vegetable oil

1 medium yellow onion, finely chopped

4 garlic cloves, minced

1 teaspoon ground turmeric

1 teaspoon salt

1 teaspoon cayenne pepper

½ teaspoon freshly ground black pepper

1 pound fresh shrimp, cleaned and peeled

2 tablespoons tomato paste

¾ cup water

½ cup finely chopped fresh cilantro

3 tablespoons bloomed saffron (see page 21)

WORTH THE WAIT Meygoo Polo (also called Havari Meygoo) is a southern Iranian dish that's spicier than typical Persian polos. It is made in different ways in different regions. The combination of cooling cilantro and shrimp and hot spices gives this dish a nice balance. It pairs well with some fresh salad. Make sure not to overcook the shrimp in the sauce, as they will get rubbery and will lose their flavor.

TO MAKE THE FILLING

1. Heat the vegetable oil in a large skillet over medium heat. When the oil begins to shimmer, add the onion and sauté until it's golden brown, about 10 minutes. Add the garlic and stir for 30 seconds or so, then stir in the turmeric, salt, cayenne, and black pepper. Cook for 1 minute or until the mixture is fragrant. Add the shrimp and toss well to coat with the spices.

2. Mix the tomato paste and water in a small bowl and pour it over the shrimp. Bring the liquid to a boil and let it simmer for 5 minutes. Add the cilantro and bloomed saffron, remove the skillet from the heat, and set the filling aside.

FOR THE RICE

6⅓ cups water, divided

2 cups long-grain white rice, such as basmati, rinsed and drained

1½ teaspoons salt

6 tablespoons vegetable oil, divided

Thin bread for the bottom of the pot (lavash works best)

TO MAKE THE RICE

1. Pour 6 cups of water into a large nonstick pot and bring it to a boil over high heat. Add the rice and salt and boil for about 10 minutes. Check one grain by pressing it between your thumb and index finger; you should be able to break the grain but the center of it should still be firm.

2. Place a colander in the sink and drain the rice. Place the pot back on the stove over medium heat. Make sure the bottom of the pot is dry. Heat 3 tablespoons of vegetable oil in the pot and arrange the bread so that it covers the bottom of the pot entirely.

3. Scoop one third of the rice into the pot and layer half the filling on top of it. Repeat with the remaining rice and filling, ending with a layer of rice. Carefully pour the remaining ⅓ cup of water around the edges of the pot. Wrap the lid in a clean towel and put it on the pot. Let the rice cook for 30 minutes, until the steam starts to escape. Pour the remaining 3 tablespoons of vegetable oil over the rice, cover, and steam for 10 minutes more or until the rice is completely tender. Serve warm.

BEYOND THE BASICS You can add ½ cup raisins and ½ cup chopped walnuts to the filling to give it some crunch and also some sweetness.

KABOBS & RICE

کباب لا پلو KABOB LA POLO

Serves 4
Prep: 15 minutes
Cook: 1 hour

FOR THE KABOBS

1 medium yellow onion

1 pound lean ground beef

1 tablespoon all-purpose flour

½ teaspoon ground turmeric

½ teaspoon freshly ground
black pepper

½ teaspoon salt

WORTH THE WAIT My maman makes Kabob la Polo whenever we are sick and need a super-nutritious, easy-to-eat meal. This dish is made of layers of rice and ground beef mixed with grated onion and seasoned with turmeric, salt, and black pepper.

TO MAKE THE KABOBS

1. Grate the onion. Squeeze it well in a clean kitchen towel or place it in a fine-mesh colander and press it with the back of a wooden spoon to extract as much liquid as possible. Discard the excess water. Transfer the onion to a large bowl.

2. Add the ground beef, flour, turmeric, pepper, and salt to the bowl with the onion. Knead the mixture with your hands until everything is well combined.

3. Wet your hands and form the meat into 8 equal-size patties. Set them aside.

FOR THE RICE

6⅓ cups water, divided

2 cups long-grain white rice, such as basmati, rinsed and drained

1½ teaspoons salt

6 tablespoons vegetable oil, divided

2 tablespoons bloomed saffron (see page 21)

1 large flour tortilla or thin bread (lavash works best) for the bottom of the pot

TO MAKE THE RICE

1. Pour 6 cups of water into a large nonstick pot and bring it to a boil over high heat. Add the rice and salt and boil for about 10 minutes. Check one grain by pressing it between your thumb and index finger; you should be able to break the grain but the center of it should still be firm.

2. Place a colander in the sink and drain the rice. Place the pot back on the stove over medium heat. Make sure the bottom of the pot is dry. Heat 3 tablespoons of vegetable oil in the pot, add the bloomed saffron, and arrange the tortilla so it covers the bottom of the pot entirely.

3. Scoop one third of the rice into the pot and place 4 meat patties on top of the rice. Repeat with the remaining rice and patties, finishing with a layer of rice. Carefully pour the remaining ⅓ cup of water around the edges of the pot. Wrap the lid in a clean towel and put it on the pot. Let the rice cook for 20 minutes, until the steam starts to escape. Pour the remaining 3 tablespoons of vegetable oil over the rice, cover, reduce the heat to low, and steam for 30 minutes or until the meat is cooked through and the rice is completely tender. Serve warm.

BEYOND THE BASICS Sprinkle a dash of sumac on the kabobs for an even more authentic flavor, and serve fresh herbs such as parsley and mint on the side.

CABBAGE & MEATBALLS MIXED RICE

 كلم پلو KALAM POLO

Serves 4
Prep: 20 minutes
Cook: 1 hour, 5 minutes

FOR THE MEATBALLS

1 small yellow onion

1 pound lean ground beef

½ teaspoon ground turmeric

½ teaspoon salt

½ teaspoon freshly ground black pepper

2 tablespoons vegetable oil

WORTH THE WAIT Kalam Polo is a hearty meal made with white cabbage, fresh tarragon and basil, and beef meatballs. The meatballs are small and can be served on the side—or just left out entirely for a vegan version of this dish.

TO MAKE THE MEATBALLS

1. Grate the onion. Squeeze it well in a clean kitchen towel or place it in a fine-mesh colander and press it with the back of a wooden spoon. Discard the excess water. Transfer the onion to a large bowl.

2. Add the ground beef, turmeric, salt, and pepper to the bowl with the grated onion. Mix well with your hands until everything is incorporated. Wet your hands and form the meat into 1-inch-diameter meatballs.

3. Heat the vegetable oil in a large skillet over medium heat. When the oil begins to shimmer, add the meatballs and cook until they are brown on all sides, 8 to 10 minutes. Remove the skillet from the heat and set aside.

FOR THE CABBAGE MIXED RICE

9 tablespoons vegetable oil, divided

1 medium yellow onion, finely chopped

3 cups shredded white cabbage

1 teaspoon ground turmeric

3 tablespoons bloomed saffron (see page 21), divided

2 teaspoons salt, divided

½ cup fresh tarragon leaves, finely chopped

1 cup fresh parsley leaves, finely chopped

1 cup fresh basil leaves, finely chopped

6⅓ cups water, divided

2 cups long-grain white rice, such as basmati, rinsed and drained

1 large flour tortilla or thin bread (lavash works well) for the bottom of the pot

MAKE IT EASIER To save time, skip making the meatballs. Just cook the ground beef with the onion and add it to the cabbage.

TO MAKE THE CABBAGE MIXED RICE

1. Heat 2 tablespoons of vegetable oil in a large skillet. When the oil begins to shimmer, add the onion and sauté until it's golden brown, about 10 minutes. Add the shredded cabbage and cook until the cabbage is tender, about 7 to 10 minutes. Add the turmeric, 1 tablespoon of bloomed saffron, and ½ teaspoon of salt. Stir and cook for 5 minutes more. Set aside.

2. In a large bowl, mix together the tarragon, parsley, and basil.

3. Meanwhile, pour 6 cups of water into a large nonstick pot and bring it to a boil over high heat. Add the rice and the remaining 1½ teaspoons of salt and boil for about 10 minutes. Check one grain by pressing it between your thumb and index finger; you should be able to break the grain but it should still be firm.

4. Place a colander in the sink and drain the rice. Place the pot back on the stove over medium heat. Make sure the bottom of the pot is dry. Heat 3 tablespoons of vegetable oil in the pot, add the remaining 2 tablespoons of bloomed saffron, and place the tortilla in the pot so it covers the bottom completely.

5. Scoop one third of the rice into the pot and layer half of the herb mixture and half of the cabbage mixture on top of the rice. Repeat with the remaining rice and fillings, finishing with a layer of rice. Carefully pour the remaining ⅓ cup of water around the edges of the pot. Wrap the lid in a clean towel and put it on the pot. Let the rice cook for 20 minutes, until the steam starts to escape. Pour the remaining 3 tablespoons of vegetable oil over the rice, cover, and steam for 10 minutes more or until the rice is completely tender. To serve, spread a layer of mixed rice on a platter and top with some meatballs. Repeat until all the rice and meatballs are used.

My Memories

When I left Iran to live in Turkey, one of the most difficult things for me was to say goodbye to my maman's cooking. Whenever I returned to Iran, I would ask my maman to make my favorite dish, Loobia Polo. When I opened the door, I would walk into

a home filled with the beautiful aroma of cinnamon and saffron, and my family waiting, making that day the best day of the year for me.

We would talk about everything that happened when we were apart, and how we'd spend our time together. At the top of the list was always Tehran's Big Bazaar, a district with many shops selling food, home appliances, and even jewelry. We bought key ingredients for all the Persian dishes we love. We'd also go to the farmers' market to get fresh produce and cookies made that morning, which were still warm.

If we had time on that visit, we also took a trip to the Khazar (Caspian) Sea in the north of Iran, where there are the most beautiful sunsets I've ever seen in my life. We'd walk on the beach, enjoying the light breeze.

When it was time for me to leave, I always left half of my heart with my family.

GREEN BEANS & BEEF MIXED RICE

لوبیا پلو LOOBIA POLO

Serves 4
Prep: 15 minutes
Cook: 1 hour, 30 minutes

FOR THE FILLING

1 pound green beans, trimmed and cut into ½-inch pieces

2 tablespoons vegetable oil

1 medium yellow onion, finely chopped

8 ounces lean ground beef

1 teaspoon ground turmeric

½ teaspoon cayenne pepper

½ teaspoon curry powder

½ teaspoon ground cinnamon

½ teaspoon salt

3 tablespoons bloomed saffron (see page 21)

2 tablespoons tomato paste

½ cup water

WORTH THE WAIT Loobia Polo is my favorite Persian dish. Thanks to a robust mix of spices—including cinnamon, curry powder, saffron, and turmeric—it has a bold, savory yet mild flavor, and I love how the rice cooks to perfection with the beef and vegetable filling.

TO MAKE THE FILLING

1. Bring a medium saucepan of water to a boil over high heat, add the green beans, and boil them for 3 to 4 minutes or until they are half cooked. Drain the beans in a colander and rinse them well under cold water. Set them aside.

2. Heat the vegetable oil in a large skillet over medium heat. When the oil begins to shimmer, add the onion and sauté until it's golden brown, about 10 minutes. Add the ground beef and cook, stirring constantly, until it is no longer pink, about 5 minutes. Add the turmeric, cayenne, and curry powder. Cook for 3 minutes, stirring constantly, until the spices release their aromas. Stir in the cinnamon, salt, and bloomed saffron.

3. In a small bowl, stir together the tomato paste, water, and green beans and pour this mixture over the beef in the skillet. Stir, reduce the heat to low, and let the mixture simmer for 5 minutes or until the sauce thickens. Remove the skillet from the heat and set it aside.

Green Beans & Beef Mixed Rice *continued*

FOR THE RICE

6⅓ cups water, divided

2 cups long-grain white rice, such as basmati, rinsed and drained

1½ teaspoons salt

6 tablespoons vegetable oil, divided

2 medium white potatoes, thinly sliced

Cucumber & Tomato Salad (page 40), for serving

TO MAKE THE RICE

1. Pour 6 cups of water into a large nonstick pot and bring it to a boil over high heat. Add the rice and salt and boil for about 7 minutes. Check one grain by pressing it between your thumb and index finger; you should be able to break the grain but it should still be hard.

2. Place a colander in the sink and drain the rice. Place the pot back on the stove over medium heat. Make sure the bottom of the pot is dry. Heat 3 tablespoons of vegetable oil in the pot and arrange the potato slices so they cover the bottom of the pot entirely.

3. Scoop one third of the rice into the pot and layer on one third of the filling. Repeat with the remaining rice and filling. Carefully pour the remaining ⅓ cup of water around the edges of the pot. Wrap the lid in a clean towel and put it on the pot. Let the rice cook for 20 minutes, until the steam starts to escape. Pour the remaining 3 tablespoons of vegetable oil over the rice, cover, reduce the heat to low, and steam for 30 minutes or until the rice is completely tender.

4. Serve with Cucumber & Tomato Salad.

COOKING TIP Make sure you don't over-boil the rice, as the filling has some water in it. The rice will cook completely when it's steamed. Check the rice after the final 30 minutes of steaming in step 3. If it is undercooked, add ⅓ cup more water, cover, and cook for 10 minutes more. Don't add too much water, as it will make the rice sticky.

FAVA BEANS & TURMERIC RICE

 دمی باقالی DAMI BAGHALI

Serves 4
Prep: 10 minutes,
plus 2 hours to soak
the beans
Cook: 1 hour, 20 minutes

2 tablespoons vegetable oil

1 medium yellow onion,
finely chopped

½ teaspoon ground turmeric

½ teaspoon cayenne pepper

2 cups dried (yellow) fava
beans, soaked in water
for 2 hours, then drained

4 cups water

1 teaspoon salt

2 cups long-grain white rice,
such as basmati, rinsed
and drained

Cucumber & Tomato Salad
(page 40), for serving

VEGAN, WORTH THE WAIT Fava beans go by many names, including broad beans and field beans. The green ones are fresh and the yellow ones are the same beans dried. In Dami Baghali, dried favas are cooked with onion, turmeric, cayenne pepper, and rice to create a satisfying side or light main dish. In my family we like it more on the mild side, but feel free to tinker with the amount of cayenne pepper to fit your preference.

1. Heat the vegetable oil in a large pot over medium heat. When the oil begins to shimmer, add the onion and sauté until it's golden brown, about 10 minutes. Stir in the turmeric and cayenne, then add the yellow fava beans and water. Bring the water to a boil and cook for 30 minutes or until the fava beans are half tender.

2. Add the salt and rice to the boiling beans and water. Cover the pot and cook over medium-low heat for 40 minutes, until the rice and beans are tender.

3. Serve warm with Cucumber & Tomato Salad.

COOKING TIP Check the rice and beans after 15 minutes and make sure there is enough water in the pot to finish cooking. If there is not enough water, add another ⅓ cup.

LENTIL & BEEF MIXED RICE

— عدس پلو ADAS POLO —

Serves 4
Prep: 15 minutes
Cook: 1 hour, 20 minutes

FOR THE FILLING

1 cup dried lentils, rinsed
and drained

2 tablespoons vegetable oil

1 onion, finely chopped

8 ounces lean ground beef

1 teaspoon ground turmeric

½ teaspoon ground cinnamon

½ teaspoon salt

2 tablespoons bloomed
saffron (see page 21)

1 cup raisins

WORTH THE WAIT Rich with lentils, raisins, dates, and ground beef, Adas Polo is a very satisfying and flavorful dish. Medjool dates are prized because they are especially large, especially sweet, and especially juicy. But if you can't find them, any dates will do. Leave out the ground beef and you will have a vegan and still very nutritious Adas Polo.

TO MAKE THE FILLING

1. Bring a medium saucepan of water to a boil over medium heat. Add the lentils and boil until they are half cooked, about 20 minutes. Drain the lentils in a colander and rinse them under cold water. Set them aside.

2. Heat the vegetable oil in a large skillet over medium heat. When the oil begins to shimmer, add the onion and sauté until it's golden brown, about 10 minutes. Add the ground beef and cook, stirring constantly, until it is no longer pink, about 5 minutes. Add the turmeric, cinnamon, salt, and bloomed saffron. Stir until the ground beef is cooked completely, 2 to 3 minutes longer. Remove the skillet from the heat and set it aside.

3. Wash the raisins and spread them out on a kitchen towel. Pat them dry, then place them in a small heatproof bowl. Set aside.

FOR THE RICE

6⅓ cups water, divided

2 cups long-grain white rice, such as basmati, rinsed and drained

1½ teaspoons salt

6 tablespoons vegetable oil, divided

2 medium white potatoes, sliced

2 tablespoons bloomed saffron (see page 21)

1 cup Medjool dates, pitted, for serving

Plain Greek yogurt, for serving

COOKING TIP Boiling the lentils with the rice for a few seconds will help distribute the lentils more evenly among the rice grains.

TO MAKE THE RICE

1. Pour 6 cups of water in a large nonstick pot and bring it to a boil over high heat. Add the rice and salt and boil for about 10 minutes. Check one grain by pressing it between your thumb and index finger; you should be able to break the grain but it should still be firm. Add the drained lentils to the pot and boil for 30 seconds.

2. Place a colander in the sink and drain the rice and lentils. Place the pot back on the stove over medium heat. Make sure the bottom of the pot is dry. Heat 3 tablespoons of vegetable oil in the pot and arrange the potato slices so they cover the bottom of the pot entirely.

3. Scoop one third of the rice into the pot and layer one third of the beef mixture on top of the rice. Repeat with the remaining rice and filling. Carefully pour the remaining ⅓ cup of water around the edges of the pot. Wrap the lid in a clean towel and put it on the pot. Let the rice cook for 20 minutes, until the steam starts to escape. Pour the remaining 3 tablespoons of vegetable oil over the rice. Place the bowl of raisins and the dates on top of the rice. Cover and steam for 10 more minutes or until the rice is completely tender.

4. In a small bowl, mix 1 cup of lentil rice with the bloomed saffron. Serve the plain lentil rice on a large platter, topped with the dates, raisins, and saffron-lentil rice.

5. Serve with plain Greek yogurt on the side.

BLACK-EYED PEAS & BEEF MIXED RICE

لوبیا چشم بلبلی پلو LOOBIA CHESHM BOLBOLI POLO

Serves 4
Prep: 15 minutes
Cook: 1 hour, 30 minutes

FOR THE FILLING

1 cup dried black-eyed peas, rinsed and drained

2 tablespoons vegetable oil

1 medium yellow onion, finely chopped

1 pound beef stew meat, cut into ½-inch cubes

1 teaspoon ground turmeric

½ teaspoon cayenne pepper

½ teaspoon curry powder

1 cup water, divided

½ teaspoon salt

3 tablespoons bloomed saffron (see page 21)

2 tablespoons tomato paste

WORTH THE WAIT Loobia Cheshm Bolboli Polo is another Persian mixed rice dish that is considered homestyle cooking around the country. As with the lentils in Lentil & Beef Mixed Rice (page 168), the peas are half cooked first, then finished off with the rice. Loobia Cheshm Bolboli Polo is delicious served with plain yogurt or Cucumber & Tomato Salad (page 40).

TO MAKE THE FILLING

1. Bring a medium saucepan of water to a boil over medium heat. Add the black-eyed peas and boil for 20 minutes, until they are half cooked. Drain the peas in a colander and rinse them under cold water. Set them aside.

2. While the peas are cooking, heat the oil in a large skillet over medium heat. When the oil begins to shimmer, add the onion and sauté until it's golden brown, about 10 minutes. Add the beef and cook, stirring constantly, until the pieces are browned on all sides, about 5 minutes. Add the turmeric, cayenne, curry powder, and ½ cup of water. Cook for 10 minutes until the beef is almost cooked through and the water has evaporated. Stir in the salt and bloomed saffron.

3. In a small bowl, stir together the tomato paste and the remaining ½ cup of water. Pour this mixture over the beef in the skillet. Stir and simmer on low for 10 minutes, until the sauce thickens and the beef is tender. Remove the skillet from the heat and set it aside.

FOR THE RICE

6⅓ cups water, divided

2 cups long-grain white rice, such as basmati, rinsed and drained

1½ teaspoons salt

6 tablespoons vegetable oil, divided

2 medium white potatoes, sliced

Plain Greek yogurt or Cucumber & Tomato Salad (page 40), for serving

TO MAKE THE RICE

1. Pour 6 cups of water into a large nonstick pot and bring it to a boil over high heat. Add the rice and salt and boil for about 7 minutes. Check one grain by pressing it between your thumb and index finger; you should be able to break the grain but it should still be hard.

2. Place a colander in the sink and drain the rice. Place the pot back on the stove over medium heat. Make sure the bottom of the pot is dry. Heat 3 tablespoons of vegetable oil in the pot and arrange the potato slices so they cover the bottom of the pot entirely.

3. Scoop one third of the rice back into the pot and layer one third of the filling on top of the rice. Repeat with the remaining rice and filling. Carefully pour the remaining ⅓ cup of water around the edges of the pot. Wrap the lid in a clean towel and put it on the pot. Let the rice cook for 20 minutes, until the steam starts to escape. Pour the remaining 3 tablespoons of vegetable oil over the rice, cover, reduce the heat to low, and steam for 30 minutes or until the rice is completely tender.

4. Serve warm with yogurt or Cucumber & Tomato Salad.

MAKE IT EASIER Use ground beef instead of stew meat to reduce the cooking time. In that case, don't add any water when you first cook the meat—just mix ½ cup of water with the tomato paste before adding it to the skillet.

MEAT & EGGPLANT SAFFRON RICE CAKE

ته چین گوشت و بادمجان TAHCHIN GOOSHT VA BADEMJAAN

Serves 4
Prep: 20 minutes
Cook: 1 hour, 40 minutes

FOR THE FILLING

4 tablespoons vegetable oil, divided

2 Japanese eggplants, thinly sliced

1 medium yellow onion, finely chopped

1 pound lean ground beef

1 teaspoon ground turmeric

2 tablespoons tomato paste

1 teaspoon salt

1 teaspoon freshly ground black pepper

1 teaspoon ground cinnamon

WORTH THE WAIT Tahchin Goosht va Bademjaan is a variation of tahchin, consisting of beef and eggplant spread between two layers of saffron-yogurt-rice mixture and then baked in the oven. It is considered a full meal all on its own, but I think it really shines alongside some fresh Cucumber & Tomato Salad (page 40).

TO MAKE THE FILLING

1. Heat 2 tablespoons of vegetable oil in a large skillet over medium heat. When the oil begins to shimmer, add the eggplant slices and cook until they are golden on both sides, about 10 minutes total. Transfer the eggplant to a plate and set aside.

2. In the same skillet, heat the remaining 2 tablespoons of vegetable oil over medium heat and sauté the onion until it's golden brown, about 10 minutes. Add the ground beef and cook, stirring constantly, until it is no longer pink, about 5 minutes. When the meat is brown, add the turmeric, tomato paste, salt, pepper, and cinnamon. Give everything a good stir and cook for 5 minutes more. Remove the skillet from the heat and set aside.

FOR THE TAHCHIN

6¼ cups water, divided

2 cups long-grain white rice, such as basmati, rinsed and drained

3½ teaspoons salt, divided

Nonstick cooking spray

1 cup plain Greek yogurt

3 large eggs

½ cup vegetable oil

4 tablespoons bloomed saffron (see page 21)

Cucumber & Tomato Salad (page 40), for serving

TO MAKE THE TAHCHIN

1. Pour 6 cups of water into a large nonstick pot and bring it to a boil over high heat. Add the rice and 1½ teaspoons of salt. Boil for about 10 minutes. Check one grain by pressing it between your thumb and index finger; you should be able to break the grain but it should still be hard in the center.

2. Preheat the oven to 350°F. Coat an 8-by- 8-inch glass baking dish with nonstick cooking spray.

3. Place a colander in the sink and drain the rice. In a large bowl, mix the rice with the yogurt, eggs, vegetable oil, remaining 1 teaspoon of salt, and the bloomed saffron. Scoop one third of the mixture into the prepared dish, cover with half of the eggplant and beef filling, add one third of the rice mixture, and cover with the remaining filling. Top with the remaining rice mixture and cover the dish with aluminum foil. Using a sharp knife, make 4 to 6 holes in the aluminum foil so the steam can escape.

4. Bake the tanchin for 1 hour or until the rice is firm and the bottom is golden brown.

5. Serve warm with Cucumber & Tomato Salad.

COOKING TIP Because this rice cake has several layers, make sure you choose a deep baking dish. A larger yet shallow baking dish would also work—just make fewer layers.

SPLIT CHICKPEA, LAMB & BARBERRY MIXED RICE

    مانی پلو MANI POLO

Serves 4
Prep: 20 minutes
Cook: 1 hour, 40 minutes

FOR THE FILLING

2 large yellow onions, divided

1 pound boneless lamb roast

4 cups water, divided

1 cup split chickpeas, rinsed and drained

2 tablespoons vegetable oil

1 cup raisins

½ cup barberries, rinsed and dried

3 tablespoons bloomed saffron (see page 21)

1 teaspoon ground turmeric

1½ teaspoons salt

½ teaspoon cayenne pepper

WORTH THE WAIT Mani Polo is a sweet-and-sour mixed rice dish that hails from the city of Damghan in northeastern Iran. Made with rice, lamb, split chickpeas, raisins, and *reshte polo*—a type of roasted noodle that you can find in Middle Eastern and Mediterranean grocery stores—it is a very filling main course and is usually served on its own.

TO MAKE THE FILLING

1. Chop 1 onion and place it in a large pot with the lamb and 2 cups of water. Bring the water to a boil over medium heat and boil the lamb until it is fully cooked and tender, 30 to 40 minutes. Discard the water and onion. Shred the lamb or just cut it into small pieces. Set aside.

2. While the lamb is cooking, combine the split chickpeas and the remaining 2 cups of water in a medium saucepan over medium heat. Bring the water to a boil and cook for about 20 minutes or until the chickpeas are tender. Drain the chickpeas in a colander and rinse them under cold water. Set aside.

3. Thinly slice the remaining onion. Heat the vegetable oil in a large skillet over medium heat. When the oil begins to shimmer, add the sliced onion and sauté until it's golden brown, about 10 minutes. Transfer the onion to a plate and set it aside. Add the raisins to the same skillet and sauté them over medium heat for about 2 minutes or until they begin to soften. Add the barberries, sauté for 1 minute, then mix in the lamb, split chickpeas, and onion. Sauté for 1 minute, then add the bloomed saffron, turmeric, salt, and cayenne. Mix and stir over medium heat for 5 minutes or until everything is well incorporated.

FOR THE RICE

6⅓ cups water, divided

2 cups long-grain white rice, such as basmati, rinsed and drained

2 ounces reshteh polo (roasted noodles)

1½ teaspoons salt

6 tablespoons vegetable oil, divided

1 large flour tortilla or thin bread (such as lavash), for the bottom of the pot

1 tablespoon ground cumin

TO MAKE THE RICE

1. Pour 6 cups of water into a large nonstick pot and bring it to a boil over high heat. Add the rice, noodles, and salt. Boil for about 10 minutes. Check one grain by pressing it between your thumb and index finger; you should be able to break the grain but it should still be firm.

2. Place a colander in the sink and drain the rice-noodle mixture. Place the pot back on the stove over medium heat. Make sure the bottom of the pot is dry. Heat 3 tablespoons of vegetable oil in the pot and place the tortilla in the pot so it covers the bottom entirely.

3. Scoop the rice back into the pot, sprinkle with the cumin, and use a spatula to push most of the rice to the middle of the pot, forming a mound. Carefully pour the remaining ⅓ cup of water around the edges of the pot. Using the end of a spatula, make 5 holes in the rice to let the steam escape. Wrap the lid in a clean towel and put it on the pot. Let the rice cook for 30 minutes, until the steam starts to escape. Pour the remaining 3 tablespoons of vegetable oil over the rice, cover, and steam for 10 minutes or until the rice is completely tender.

4. To serve, spread a layer of rice and noodles on a large platter, top it with a layer of filling, and repeat the layers until everything is used. Serve warm.

COOKING TIP Make sure the rice is fully cooked before serving. If the rice is still hard and not cooked after the first 30 minutes of steaming, pour ⅓ cup water around the edge of the pot and proceed as in step 3.

LAMB & BARBERRY MIXED RICE

قیمه نثار GHEIMEH NESAR

Serves 6
Prep: 45 minutes
Cook: 2 hours, 30 minutes

FOR THE FILLING

2 pounds boneless leg of lamb, cut into 1-inch cubes

2 medium yellow onions, finely chopped, divided

4 tablespoons vegetable oil, divided

1 teaspoon ground turmeric

½ teaspoon ground cardamom

¼ teaspoon ground cumin

3 cups water

2 tablespoons unsalted butter

¾ cup barberries, rinsed and dried

1 tablespoon candied orange peel

⅓ cup chopped unsalted pistachios, divided

⅓ cup slivered almonds, divided

½ teaspoon salt

⅓ cup bloomed saffron (see page 21)

½ teaspoon ground cinnamon

1 tablespoon tomato paste

3 tablespoons rosewater

WORTH THE WAIT Gheimeh Nesar is from the city of Ghazvin, which is near the capital city of Tehran. This dish is sweet with candied orange peel, tart with barberries, and savory with lamb—all refined with plenty of saffron. The entire Persian palate (and pantry!) is in this dish.

TO MAKE THE FILLING

1. Combine the lamb, 1 chopped onion, and 2 tablespoons of vegetable oil in a large pot over medium heat. Cook until the lamb juice is released and it starts simmering slowly, about 20 minutes. Add the turmeric, cardamom, and cumin. Stir well and add the water. Cover and cook for 45 minutes, until the lamb is very tender and is easily shredded with a fork.

2. In a large pan, heat the remaining 2 tablespoons of vegetable oil over medium heat. When the oil begins to shimmer, add the remaining onion and sauté until it's golden brown, about 10 minutes. Reduce the heat to low and add the butter and barberries. Stir constantly until the butter melts and the barberries are shiny, about 5 minutes. Stir in the candied orange peel, then half of the pistachios and half of the almonds. Mix well. Reserve the rest of the nuts for garnish.

3. When the lamb is fully cooked, add the onion and barberry mixture, salt, bloomed saffron, cinnamon, and tomato paste to the pot. Stir well until everything is combined. Simmer until the sauce is thick, about 15 minutes. Add the rosewater and remove the pot from the heat.

FOR THE RICE

6⅓ cups water, divided

3 cups long-grain white rice, such as basmati, rinsed and drained

1½ teaspoons salt

6 tablespoons vegetable oil, divided

1 large flour tortilla or thin bread (such as lavash), for the bottom of the pot

1 tablespoon unsalted butter

2 tablespoons barberries, rinsed and dried

2 tablespoons bloomed saffron (see page 21)

COOKING TIP To save time, make the rice while the lamb is cooking. You can also sauté the onion and barberries while the lamb and rice are cooking, so they will be ready to be added to the lamb when it's fully cooked.

TO MAKE THE RICE

1. Pour 6 cups of water into a large nonstick pot and bring it to a boil over high heat. Add the rice and salt and boil for about 10 minutes. Check one grain by pressing it between your thumb and index finger; you should be able to break the grain but it should still be firm.

2. Place a colander in the sink and drain the rice. Place the pot back on the stove over medium heat. Make sure the bottom of the pot is dry. Heat 3 tablespoons of vegetable oil in the pot and place the tortilla in the pot so it covers the bottom entirely.

3. Scoop the rice into the pot. Use a spatula to push most of the rice to the middle of the pot, forming a mound. Carefully pour the remaining ⅓ cup of water around the edges of the pot. Using the edge of a spatula, make 5 holes in the surface of the rice to let the steam escape. Wrap the lid in a clean towel and put it on the pot. Let the rice cook for 30 minutes, until the steam starts to escape. Pour the remaining 3 tablespoons of vegetable oil over the rice, cover, and steam for 10 minutes or until the rice is completely tender.

4. Melt the butter in a small saucepan and sauté the barberries until they are shiny, about 5 minutes. Set aside.

5. In a small bowl, mix 4 tablespoons of cooked rice with the bloomed saffron. Set aside.

6. To serve, spread one third of the rice in a layer on a large platter and top with half of the filling. Top with another third of the rice and the remaining filling. Spread the last layer of the rice over the filling and decorate the Gheimeh Nesar with the saffron rice mixture, barberries, and the reserved pistachios and almonds.

JEWELED SWEET RICE

مرصع پلو — MORASA POLO

Serves 4
Prep: 45 minutes
Cook: 1 hour, 10 minutes

FOR THE FILLING

2 oranges

1 cup water

1 cup sugar

2 carrots, peeled
and julienned

3 tablespoons vegetable oil

1 medium yellow onion,
finely chopped

½ teaspoon ground turmeric

½ cup barberries, rinsed
and dried

½ cup raisins

½ teaspoon salt

¼ teaspoon ground
cardamom

½ cup ground unsalted
pistachios

⅓ cup slivered almonds

3 tablespoons bloomed
saffron (see page 21)

¼ teaspoon ground cumin

VEGAN, WORTH THE WAIT This beautiful Persian dish is adorned with slivered almonds, pistachios, barberries, and candied carrot and orange peel, and is usually served at weddings and celebrations. Compared to other Persian rice dishes, Morasa Polo requires more work. That's why it is a party dish. You can serve it with a savory dish, such as Saffron Chicken (page 100), or offer it as a unique dessert.

TO MAKE THE FILLING

1. Peel the oranges. Cut the peel into very thin matchsticks, making sure not to get any of the bitter white pith. Wash the sliced orange peel three times with cold water, then pat it dry in a clean kitchen towel. Combine the water and sugar in a medium saucepan over medium heat, and stir until the sugar is completely dissolved. When the syrup begins to boil, add the orange peel and carrots. Stir gently and cook for 10 minutes, then remove the pan from the heat. (Eat the oranges while you're cooking!)

2. Heat the vegetable oil in a large skillet over medium heat. When the oil begins to shimmer, add the onion and sauté until it's golden brown, about 10 minutes. Add the turmeric, reduce the heat to low, and stir in the barberries and raisins. Stir well until the fruits are shiny. Take the orange peel and carrots out of the syrup and add them to the barberries and raisins. Stir in the salt, cardamom, pistachios, and almonds. Give it a good stir, then add 2 tablespoons of sugar syrup to the mixture. Add the bloomed saffron and cumin. Stir well, remove the skillet from the heat, and set it aside.

FOR THE RICE

6⅓ cups water, divided

2 cups long-grain white rice, such as basmati, rinsed and drained

1½ teaspoons salt

6 tablespoons vegetable oil, divided

1 large flour tortilla or thin bread (such as lavash), for the bottom of the pot

TO MAKE THE RICE

1. Pour 6 cups of water into a large nonstick pot and bring it to a boil over high heat. Add the rice and salt and boil for about 10 minutes. Check one grain by pressing it between your thumb and index finger; you should be able to break the grain but it should still be firm.

2. Place a colander in the sink and drain the rice. Place the pot back on the stove over medium heat. Make sure the bottom of the pot is dry. Heat 3 tablespoons of vegetable oil in the pot and place the tortilla in the pot so it covers the bottom entirely.

3. Scoop the rice into the center of the pot, creating a mound. Carefully pour the remaining ⅓ cup of water around the rice along the edges of the pot. Using the end of a spatula, make 5 holes in the rice to let the steam escape. Wrap the lid in a clean towel and put it on the pot. Let the rice cook for 30 minutes, until the steam starts to escape. Pour the remaining 3 tablespoons of vegetable oil over the rice, cover, and steam for 10 minutes or until the rice is completely tender.

4. On a large platter, spread one third of the cooked rice and layer one third of the barberry and pistachio filling on top. Repeat with the remaining rice and filling, using the last layer of filling to decorate the dish. Serve warm.

COOKING TIP It's important to make sure that the bitter white parts of the orange peel don't end up in the dish. Also, taste the filling before adding the syrup in step 3. If it's sweet enough, there is no need to add the syrup.

8 DRINKS

YOGURT DRINK

دوغ DOOGH

Serves 6
Prep: 10 minutes

2 cups plain yogurt

1 tablespoon dried mint

1½ teaspoons salt

5 cups water

VEGETARIAN, QUICK & EASY Doogh is probably the most common drink served with food in Persian cuisine. At its simplest, it's made from just three ingredients: yogurt, water, and salt. Dried mint is now a common addition. To make carbonated doogh, substitute 2 cups of carbonated water for the still water. This refreshing drink pairs very well with kabobs and other big pieces of meat.

1. Mix the yogurt, dried mint, and salt in a pitcher using a large fork. Slowly add the water, stirring constantly, until the water and yogurt are completely combined.

2. Fill six glasses with some ice and pour the Doogh over the ice in each glass.

3. Serve with any savory dish except fish.

MAKE IT EASIER To make the Doogh extra smooth, combine the ingredients in a blender and purée. Dried mint will combine better with yogurt if it's blended, and this way the Doogh won't have any lumps.

ROSEWATER SYRUP & DRINK

شربت گلاب SHARBAT GOLAB

Serves 6
Prep: 10 minutes
Cook: 10 minutes

FOR THE ROSEWATER SYRUP

2 cups sugar

2 cups water

¼ cup rosewater

FOR THE DRINK

¼ cup rosewater syrup

½ cup ice

1 cup water

VEGAN, QUICK & EASY Sharbat Golab is a basic syrup that is used widely in Persian drinks, desserts, and pastries. Its sweetness and flavor can be adjusted according to your taste; just add more water to make it less sweet, or squeeze in a few drops of freshly squeezed lemon juice for an even more refreshing taste. You can find rosewater at Middle Eastern and Indian markets.

TO MAKE THE ROSEWATER SYRUP

1. Combine the sugar and water in a medium saucepan over medium heat. Bring the mixture to a boil, then reduce the heat to low and simmer for 10 minutes.

2. Stir in the rosewater and simmer for 1 more minute. Turn off the heat and let the syrup cool completely before using. Store it in a jar in the refrigerator for up to 2 weeks.

TO MAKE THE DRINK

1. In a tall glass, combine the rosewater syrup and ice.

2. Pour in the water and stir until well combined.

WHY IT WORKS You add the rosewater at the end to keep its delicate aroma, which is easily cooked away.

SAFFRON SYRUP & DRINK

شربت زعفران SHARBAT ZAFERAN

Serves 6
Prep: 5 minutes
Cook: 25 minutes

FOR THE SAFFRON SYRUP

1½ cups sugar

2 cups water

¼ cup bloomed
saffron (see page 21)

2 tablespoons rosewater

FOR THE DRINK

¼ cup saffron syrup

½ cup ice

1 cup water

VEGAN, QUICK & EASY Sharbat Zaferan is a syrup made of sugar, water, and saffron. In my family, we also add rosewater. A drink made with this syrup is perfect for summer days, as it is very refreshing and delicious. On hot days, Sharbat Zaferan is served to guests instead of tea in many Iranian households.

TO MAKE THE SAFFRON SYRUP

1. Combine the sugar and water in a medium saucepan over medium heat. Bring the mixture to a boil, then reduce the heat to low and let it simmer for 10 minutes.

2. Stir in the bloomed saffron and simmer for another 15 minutes. Stir in the rosewater, remove the pan from the heat, and let the syrup cool completely before using. Store it in a jar in the refrigerator for up to 1 week.

TO MAKE THE DRINK

1. In a tall glass, combine the saffron syrup and ice.

2. Pour in the water and stir until well combined.

BEYOND THE BASICS **Add a couple of whole cardamom pods to the syrup to give it an even more complex flavor. Just take the pods out of the syrup before you pour it into a jar.**

MINT SYRUP & DRINK

شربت نعنا SHARBAT NA'NAA

Serves 8
Prep: 5 minutes
Cook: 35 minutes

FOR THE MINT SYRUP

2 cups water

2 cups fresh mint
leaves, rinsed

1 cup sugar

FOR THE DRINK

¼ cup mint syrup

½ cup ice

1 cup water

VEGAN We always make a large batch of this syrup to use during the summer. Sharbat Na'naa is an excellent warm-weather drink because it prevents dehydration. For this syrup, fresh mint and water are first boiled together, and we use less sugar than in other syrups, so the minty flavor really shines through.

TO MAKE THE MINT SYRUP

1. Combine the water and mint in a medium saucepan over medium heat. Bring the mixture to a boil, then reduce the heat to low and let it simmer for 20 minutes.

2. Set a colander over a small saucepan and pour the water and mint through the colander. Discard the mint leaves.

3. Place the pan with the mint water over medium heat. Add the sugar and simmer for 15 minutes, stirring frequently. Turn off the heat and let the syrup cool completely before using. Store it in a jar in the refrigerator for up to 2 weeks.

TO MAKE THE DRINK

1. In a tall glass, combine the mint syrup and ice.

2. Pour in the water and stir until well combined.

INGREDIENT TIP Use fresh spearmint, peppermint, wintergreen, or whatever mint variety you like—or a combination.

MINT & VINEGAR SYRUP & DRINK

شربت سکنجبین SHARBAT SEKANJABIN

Serves 8
Prep: 5 minutes
Cook: 25 minutes

FOR THE SYRUP

2 cups sugar

2 cups water

½ cup white vinegar

1½ cups fresh mint leaves, rinsed

VEGAN, QUICK & EASY Sharbat Sekanjabin is my favorite drink. It's very refreshing because the syrup is infused with a lot of fresh mint. The vinegar in this syrup gives a nice tanginess to the syrup, so it's not overly sweet and is perfect for hot days. Many families have beautiful memories associated with this syrup, as it's a must for the thirteenth day of spring (Sizdah Bedar, the Festival of Joy and Solidarity), when everyone goes on a picnic.

TO MAKE THE SYRUP

1. Combine the sugar and water in a medium saucepan over medium heat. Bring the mixture to a boil, then reduce the heat to low and let it simmer for 10 minutes.

2. Add the white vinegar and simmer for another 15 minutes. Turn off the heat, drop the mint into the syrup, cover, and let the syrup cool completely.

3. Take the mint out and pour the syrup into a jar. Keep the jar in the refrigerator for up to 10 days.

FOR THE DRINK

⅓ cup mint and vinegar syrup

½ cup ice

1 cup water

TO MAKE THE DRINK

1. In a tall glass, combine the mint and vinegar syrup and ice.

2. Pour in the water and stir until well combined.

BEYOND THE BASICS Another version of this drink is Khiar Sekanjabin—cucumber, mint, and vinegar drink. To make this version, grate 1 cucumber and place it in a tall glass. Add the vinegar and mint syrup and ice, then fill the glass with water and give it a stir.

MINT & CINNAMON DRINK

دمنوش نعنا و دارچین DAMNOOSHE NA'NAA VA DARCHIN

Serves 4
Prep: 5 minutes
Cook: 7 minutes

1 cup fresh mint leaves, rinsed

2 cinnamon sticks

4 cups water

VEGAN, QUICK & EASY Damnooshe Na'naa va Darchin keeps many Iranians hydrated during the month of Ramadan, when we fast during the daylight hours. It is not typically sweet but can be sweetened with simple syrup or sugar if you like. This versatile drink can be served either hot or cold with ice.

1. Place the mint and cinnamon sticks in a large teapot. Bring the water to a boil and pour it over the mint and cinnamon. Cover and let the mixture steep for 7 minutes.

2. Carefully remove the mint and cinnamon sticks from the teapot.

3. Pour the drink into cups and serve hot or over ice.

COOKING TIP Hot or cold, this drink should be served immediately for the best taste.

SAFFRON & ROSE TEA

چای زعفران و گل CHAI ZAFERAN VA GOL

Serves 2
Prep: 5 minutes
Cook: 10 minutes

3 tablespoons loose-leaf
black tea

Water

4 saffron strands

3 dried Persian rose petals

VEGAN, QUICK & EASY This is a beloved variation on Persian brewed tea that brings back so many memories for me. With the additions of saffron strands and dried Persian rose petals, it has a beautiful flavor and aroma and is great for relaxation and comfort. You'll find the rose petals at Middle Eastern grocery stores and online.

1. Place the tea in a teapot, preferably one that has a strainer inside.

2. Pour some water into the teapot and rinse the tea. Discard the water, leaving the wet tea leaves inside the teapot, then add the saffron strands and dried rose petals. Set the teapot aside.

3. Fill a kettle with cold water and bring it to a boil over medium heat. Pour the boiling water into the teapot and secure the lid. Place the kettle back over medium heat and set the teapot on top. (You may need to remove the lid of the kettle to do this.) Cover the teapot with a small cloth to keep it warm and turn the heat to low. Let the tea brew for 5 to 10 minutes.

4. Fill half of each cup with brewed tea and then top up the cups with hot water.

5. Serve the tea hot with raisins, dried fruit, or dates on the side.

COOKING TIP The saffron strands and dried Persian rose petals are added after rinsing the tea in order to retain their colors and flavors.

PERSIAN BREWED TEA

چای دم کرده CHAI DAM KARDEH

Serves 2
Prep: 5 minutes
Cook: 10 minutes

3 tablespoons loose-leaf black tea

Water

BEYOND THE BASICS
Always use cold water to brew tea for a better color and appearance. To keep the tea warmer for a longer time, rinse the teacups with hot water.

VEGAN, QUICK & EASY Tea to Iranians is like coffee to those in other cultures—a very essential part of daily life. Persian brewed tea is strong, and is usually mixed with more water before serving. Any type of black tea will work—it needs to be loose leaf, not a teabag, because loose-leaf tea brews slower and better in hot water.

1. Place the tea in a teapot, preferably one that has a strainer inside.

2. Pour some water into the teapot and rinse the tea. Discard the water, leaving the wet tea leaves inside the teapot.

3. Fill a kettle with cold water and bring it to a boil over medium heat. Pour the boiling water into the teapot and secure the lid. Place the kettle back over medium heat and set the teapot on top. (You may need to remove the lid of the kettle to do this.) Cover the teapot with a small cloth to keep it warm and turn the heat to low. Let the tea brew for 5 to 10 minutes.

4. Fill half of each cup with brewed tea and then top up the cups with hot water.

5. Serve the tea hot with raisins, dried fruit, or dates on the side.

My Memories

Whether it's the traditional samovar and teapot, or a kettle on the stove top with a teapot on top, or a modern electric tea maker, there is always some sort of tea brewing apparatus in every Iranian household anywhere in the world.

Tea is very important to Iranians—there is no way around it. Fresh-brewed tea is a necessity, and no one would enjoy drinking brewed tea that has been sitting on the stove for a long time. Nowadays, there are many different types of tea in Iran, but in olden days, there was only black tea and no tea bags.

Iranians like their tea in glass cups, so the color is set to their desire. Some like their tea light and some like it dark; you adjust that by varying how much tea you pour in the cup and how much hot water you top it off with. My recommendation is to always have it more on the red side than on the dark brown side, because it tastes better that way.

CARDAMOM & ROSEWATER TEA

چای هل و گلاب CHAI HEL VA GOLAB

Serves 2
Prep: 5 minutes
Cook: 10 minutes

3 tablespoons loose-leaf black tea

Water

4 whole green cardamom pods

1 tablespoon rosewater

VEGAN, QUICK & EASY Another variation of Persian brewed tea, this cardamom and rosewater drink is a wonderful way to welcome guests to your home. Cardamom and rosewater are both used in many Persian desserts, and therefore this tea would pair well with sweets.

1. Place the tea in a teapot, preferable one that has a strainer inside.

2. Pour some water into the teapot and rinse the tea. Discard the water, leaving the wet tea leaves inside the teapot, then add the cardamom pods. Set the teapot aside.

3. Fill a kettle with cold water and bring it to a boil over medium heat. Pour the boiling water into the teapot and secure the lid. Place the kettle back over medium heat and set the teapot on top. (You may need to remove the lid of the kettle to do this.) Cover the teapot with a small cloth to keep it warm and turn the heat to low. Let the tea brew for 5 minutes, then add the rosewater and brew for another 5 minutes.

4. Fill half of each cup with brewed cardamom and rosewater tea, then top up the cups with hot water.

5. Serve the tea hot with raisins, dried fruit, or dates on the side.

COOKING TIP Add the rosewater right before serving so the aroma remains strong. This tea must be used immediately, as rosewater will lose its aroma if the tea stays in the pot for a long time.

BANANA & DATE ENERGY SMOOTHIE

معجون MAJOON

Serves 2
Prep: 10 minutes

1 cup cold whole milk

4 tablespoons vanilla
ice cream

2 ripe bananas, peeled
and sliced

⅓ cup chopped walnuts

⅓ cup unsalted pistachios

1 tablespoon unsweetened
shredded coconut

1 tablespoon rosewater

½ teaspoon ground cinnamon

8 Medjool dates, pitted
and peeled

VEGETARIAN, QUICK & EASY Majoon is a very tasty drink made with ripe bananas, dates, milk, and sometimes coconut. This is a smoothie that will keep you full for hours and is ready in no time. Choose the nuts you like the best—you can substitute almonds, hazelnuts, or even sesame seeds. Some people like to add a couple of spoonsful of heavy cream; if you do, leave the ice cream out. No matter what, I always add a dash of cinnamon, as it goes well with bananas and dates.

1. Put the milk and vanilla ice cream in a blender. Add the bananas, walnuts, pistachios, coconut, rosewater, cinnamon, and dates.

2. Blend for 1 minute or until everything is smooth and well combined.

3. Serve cold.

INGREDIENT TIP To peel the dates easily, first soak them in hot water for 10 minutes.

9 DESSERTS & SWEET TREATS

RICE FLOUR PUDDING

Serves 4
Prep: 5 minutes
Cook: 25 minutes

2 cups whole milk

½ cup water

4 tablespoons sugar

3 tablespoons rice flour

1 tablespoon rosewater

VEGETARIAN, QUICK & EASY Fereni is an Iranian pudding made from rice flour, milk, sugar, and rosewater. You'll find rice flour at Asian and Middle Eastern markets, health food stores, and even some supermarkets (try the gluten-free aisle). Since it's mostly milk, this pudding is a good breakfast dish for kids and a great starter for Iftar, the sunset meal during Ramadan. Fereni can be served cold or warm, and tastes great with a dash of cinnamon. Once you master the basic technique, you can add any additional flavors to the Fereni, such as chocolate, saffron, or cardamom.

1. Pour the milk, water, and sugar into a small saucepan and place it over medium heat. Stir until the mixture is warm and the sugar is completely dissolved, about 5 minutes.

2. Turn off the heat. Using a ladle, pour ½ cup of the milk and water mixture into a bowl and add the rice flour to it. Whisk the flour into the liquid, making sure there are no lumps.

3. Add the rice flour mixture to the pan and turn the heat back to medium. Stir constantly until the pudding is thick and well blended, 15 to 20 minutes.

4. Stir in the rosewater and cook for 1 minute more.

5. Pour the pudding into small individual bowls. Serve it warm or cold.

WHY IT WORKS Mixing rice flour with milk before adding it to the pot will keep the rice flour from turning into lumps.

RICE PUDDING

Serves 4
Prep: 10 minutes,
plus overnight
to soak the rice
Cook: 1 hour, 30 minutes

1 cup short-grain white rice,
soaked in water overnight

2 cups water

4 cups whole milk,
at room temperature

½ cup sugar

3 tablespoons rosewater

1 teaspoon ground cardamom

VEGETARIAN, WORTH THE WAIT Persian rice pudding is a little bit different than those made in other cultures, as it's not very sweet on its own and is usually served cold, topped with jam or molasses. I recommend having it with some maple syrup. Make sure you use short-grain rice for this recipe, as longer grains won't produce the same soft texture.

1. Drain the rice. Put it in a large pot with the water over medium heat. Bring the water to a boil, reduce the heat to low, and simmer, half-covered, until the rice is almost tender, about 30 minutes.

2. Gradually stir in the milk and sugar and continue cooking, uncovered, until the rice is very soft, about 40 minutes. Stir the pudding occasionally while it's cooking to prevent it from sticking to the bottom of the pot.

3. Add the rosewater and ground cardamom, stir, and cook for 10 minutes more. Turn off the heat, cover the pot, and let it sit for 10 minutes.

4. Spoon the pudding into small individual bowls and refrigerate until chilled. Serve cold with jam or molasses.

BEYOND THE BASICS **For saffron rice pudding, add 2 tablespoons bloomed saffron at the very end.**

COCONUT SWEETS

لوز نارگیل LOZ-E NARGIL

Serves 8
Prep: 15 minutes,
plus 2 to 3 hours
for chilling
Cook: 15 minutes

1 cup sugar

½ cup water

¼ cup rosewater

2½ cups unsweetened
shredded coconut,
plus 2 tablespoons

Ground unsalted pistachios
(optional)

VEGAN Loz-e Nargil is a simple Iranian treat made of unsweetened coconut, sugar, water, and rosewater. It's always best to let it stay in the fridge for a couple of hours before serving, so it's easier to cut into pieces. Loz-e Nargil is commonly served for the New Year and other celebrations. It has the consistency of fudge with a semi-sweet, coconutty flavor.

1. Mix the sugar and water in a medium saucepan and place it over medium heat. Cook until the sugar is melted and dissolved, about 5 minutes, then stir in the rosewater. Cook for another 10 minutes or until the syrup starts to thicken. Turn off the heat and let the syrup cool for 10 minutes. Using a wire whisk, beat the syrup for 2 minutes.

2. Place 2½ cups of shredded coconut in a large bowl and pour the syrup over the coconut. Using a wooden spoon, stir everything together until the mixture resembles a soft dough. Sprinkle the remaining 2 tablespoons of shredded coconut on the bottom of an 8-by- 8-inch glass baking dish and spread the coconut dough over it. Cover and chill the Loz-e Nargil in the refrigerator for 2 to 3 hours before serving.

3. To serve, cut the sweets into diamonds and top them with ground pistachios (if using).

BEYOND THE BASICS If desired, add 2 tablespoons bloomed saffron to the mixture while cooking. You can also add 1 teaspoon ground cardamom for an even deeper flavor.

DATE DESSERT

 رنگینک RANGINAK

Serves 6
Prep: 20 minutes,
plus 2 hours for chilling
Cook: 10 minutes

30 Medjool dates, pitted

1 cup whole, unsalted shelled walnuts

2 sticks unsalted butter

2 cups all-purpose flour

1 teaspoon ground cinnamon

1 teaspoon ground cardamom

2 tablespoons powdered sugar

2 tablespoons ground pistachios (optional)

Persian Brewed Tea (page 190), for serving

COOKING TIP Flour burns quickly over the heat. Stir it constantly to prevent burning, and once it's golden brown, immediately take the pan off the heat.

VEGETARIAN Ranginak is a sort of stuffed date crumble that hails from the south of Iran. Since dates are the stars of this dish, it's important that you source large, plump quality ones that are not dry. This dessert is very nutritious with a wonderful, earthy-sweet flavor from the cinnamon and cardamom. Ranginak is a must in many Iranian households during Ramadan, because a small portion keeps you full for some time.

1. Stuff all the dates with walnuts, putting them in the cavity where the pit was. Try not to break the dates. Place them in a single layer in a pie plate or other shallow dish; set aside.

2. Melt the butter in a small saucepan over medium heat and sift in the flour. Using a wooden spoon, stir constantly until the mixture turns golden brown, 5 to 8 minutes. Stir in the cinnamon and cardamom. Remove the pan from the heat and set it aside. Let the mixture cool for 5 to 10 minutes.

3. Pour the flour and butter mixture over the dates, making sure it covers the dates.

4. Place the dish in the refrigerator for 2 hours or until the top is set.

5. Sprinkle the powdered sugar and pistachios (if using) over the top.

6. Serve cold with Persian brewed tea.

HONEY CANDY

سوهان عسلی SOHAN ASALI

Serves 8
Prep: 10 minutes
Cook: 10 minutes

½ cup sugar

1 tablespoon honey

2 tablespoons vegetable oil

1 teaspoon bloomed saffron (see page 21)

½ cup mixed unsalted nuts

VEGETARIAN, QUICK & EASY Sohan Asali is one of the most famous candies we make for Persian New Year, Norooz. It's made with caramelized sugar, honey, saffron, and different types of nuts or seeds—any mixture of slivered almonds, sesame seeds, cashews, pistachios, walnuts, etc. The most important part of making these candies is to cook the sugar and honey so the candies are crispy and not chewy. It sometimes takes a couple of tries to get it right, but it's defintely worth it.

1. Line two baking sheets with parchment paper; set aside.

2. Put the sugar, honey, and vegetable oil in a small saucepan over medium heat and cook, stirring, until the sugar starts to caramelize, 5 to 7 minutes. Tilt the saucepan so the sugar melts evenly.

3. When the sugar is completely melted and the mixture begins to simmer, lower the heat and add the bloomed saffron and nuts. Stir a couple of times so everything is fully combined, but don't stir the candy mixture too much, or the oil will separate from the sugar.

4. Test the readiness of the candy by dropping a little bit of it into cold water. If it hardens into a crispy ball, it's ready. The color should be deep golden brown. Turn off the heat.

5. Using a small spoon, quickly drop the candies onto the parchment paper in spoonfuls. Be quick, because the mixture will start to harden. Let the candies harden at room temperature for 10 to 15 minutes before serving

MAKE IT EASIER To clean the saucepan, fill it with water and place it over high heat. Bring the water to a boil and stir with a wooden spoon until the remaining hardened candy has dissolved.

SOFT ROSEWATER CANDY

باسلوق BASLOGH

Serves 8
Prep: 15 minutes
Cook: 15 minutes

1½ cups wheat starch

2½ cups water

¼ cup rosewater

1 cup sugar

½ tablespoon unsalted butter

1 cup unsweetened shredded coconut

½ cup walnut halves

VEGETARIAN, QUICK & EASY Baslogh is a soft candy that is made for the longest night of the year, Shab-e Yalda, and also for New Year. It's not overly sweet, and it's covered with shredded coconut, which gives it a fresh and tropical taste. This candy is made with wheat starch, which can be found in health food stores and Asian and Middle Eastern supermarkets. To make saffron Baslogh, add 2 tablespoons of bloomed saffron to the mixture while it's cooking.

1. Mix together the wheat starch, water, and rosewater in a medium saucepan until the wheat starch has dissolved. Put the pan over medium heat and add the sugar and butter. Stir constantly and cook until the mixture is thick and turns into a paste, 15 to 20 minutes. Turn off the heat and set the paste aside.

2. Spread the shredded coconut on a plate. Use a spoon to roll up a small ball of the paste, then drop it into the coconut and roll until it's completely coated.

3. Place the ball on a serving plate and press a walnut half on top. Repeat with the remaining paste, coconut, and walnut halves.

4. Store the candies in an airtight container in the refrigerator for up to 1 week.

COOKING TIP As the paste is quite soft, you might need to use your hands to form it into balls, or coat the spoon lightly with nonstick cooking spray.

PERSIAN ROSETTES

نان پنجره ای NAN PANJEREH-I

Serves 6
Prep: 5 minutes, plus
30 minutes for resting
Cook: 30 minutes

⅓ cup wheat starch

4 tablespoons rosewater

3 large eggs

⅓ cup all-purpose flour

½ cup vegetable oil for frying,
plus more if needed

Powdered sugar

COOKING TIP If the oil is not hot enough, the batter will stick to the iron, and if the oil is too hot, the rosettes will quickly burn. Adjust the heat as necessary to keep the oil at a steady temperature throughout the frying process.

VEGETARIAN These rosewater-flavored cookies are made with wheat starch, which makes them very crispy, and a dusting of powdered sugar gives them just a hint of sweetness. To make the rosettes, you need a special rosette iron, which can be found in baking stores or online.

1. Mix together the wheat starch and rosewater in a large bowl until it forms a paste. Add the eggs and beat until they are fully combined. Add the flour and mix until the batter is smooth. Let the batter sit at room temperature for 30 minutes before frying.

2. Heat the oil in a small saucepan until bubbles form around a toothpick touching the bottom of the pan. Heat the rosette iron by putting it in the hot oil for 10 seconds. Lift the iron, shake off the excess oil, and immediately dip it into the batter, just enough so that the edge of the iron is even with the surface of the batter. There shouldn't be any batter on the upper surface of the iron. Once the iron is coated with batter, dip it back into the hot oil, let the rosette puff and drop off the iron, and then take the iron out of the oil.

3. Using tongs or chopsticks, fry the rosette on each side for 30 seconds or until golden brown. Immediately remove the rosette from the oil and place it on paper towels to drain.

4. Repeat with the remaining batter. When all the rosettes are ready, let them cool a bit, then dust them with powdered sugar.

My Memories

In our family, and in many other Iranian families, Norooz is a very special occasion. The holiday preparations start weeks before and continue for 13 days after the actual Persian New Year. We always make our own cookies to give to friends and

family, because Norooz is all about getting together, cherishing the arrival of a new year, and looking forward to nature being born again.

Every year we start preparing for Norooz by growing sabzeh—wheat or lentil sprouts—until they are completely green. Then we bake cookies, such as Shirini Nokhodchi and Nan Berenji. Everyone cleans their homes, and people buy new clothes. On New Year's Day, and for days after that, families visit each other and have a wonderful time together.

Today, it doesn't matter what part of the world we live in; in my family, we always try to be together on New Year's Day.

ROASTED CHICKPEA FLOUR COOKIES

شیرینی نخودچی SHIRINI NOKHODCHI

Serves 10
Prep: 20 minutes,
plus overnight to chill
Cook: 15 minutes

9 ounces vegetable
shortening

2 cups powdered sugar

1 pound roasted
chickpea flour

1 teaspoon ground cardamom

2 tablespoons
all-purpose flour

1 tablespoon ground
pistachios

VEGAN Shirini Nokhodchi is one of the most beloved cookies in Iran, essentially a sugar cookie with chickpea flour, cardamom, and ground pistachios. It is specifically baked for the Persian New Year, Norooz. Because the dough does not contain eggs, it can be particularly delicate and difficult to work with, and the cookies might fall apart if you handle them too much when they come out of the oven. For best results, roll these cookies out in small batches and let them cool completely before moving them to a serving plate. Traditionally, we use a small clover-shaped cookie cutter for Shirini Nokhodchi, but you can use whatever cookie cutters you have on hand.

1. Combine the shortening and powdered sugar in a large bowl and beat the mixture with an electric mixer or a wire whisk until it turns a light cream color.

2. Add the chickpea flour, cardamom, and all-purpose flour to the bowl and stir gently until all the ingredients are well incorporated.

3. Divide the dough in half and shape each half into a disk. Wrap the disks in plastic and refrigerate the dough for at least 12 or up to 24 hours.

4. Preheat the oven to 350°F. Line two baking sheets with parchment paper.

5. Take the dough out of the refrigerator and let it sit for 15 minutes to come to room temperature. Dust just a little flour on a rolling pin and roll out one dough disk to a ½-inch thickness. Use a cookie cutter to cut it into shapes. Place the cookies on one of the prepared baking sheets. Repeat with the second disk.

6. Sprinkle the ground pistachios over the cookies. Bake for 15 minutes, until the bottoms are very light brown. Remove the cookies from the oven and let them cool on the baking sheets for about 20 minutes, then transfer them to a serving plate.

7. These cookies will stay fresh in an airtight container for up to 10 days.

INGREDIENT TIP Roasted chickpea flour is not the same as regular chickpea flour. You can find roasted chickpea flour in Persian supermarkets or online.

COCONUT COOKIES

شیرینی نارگیلی SHIRINI NARGILI

Serves 6
Prep: 5 minutes
Cook: 12 minutes

2 egg whites

4 tablespoons
granulated sugar

2 cups unsweetened
shredded coconut

VEGETARIAN, QUICK & EASY Shirini Nargili is one of my favorite cookies to make for Norooz. These cookies are filled with unsweetened shredded coconut and are somewhat similar to coconut macaroons. The cookies are soft and chewy, and they can stay fresh in an airtight container for up to a week.

1. Preheat the oven to 325°F. Line two baking sheets with parchment paper.

2. In a large bowl, beat the egg whites with an electric mixer or a wire whisk until they're foamy. Gradually add the sugar and beat on high until stiff peaks form.

3. Using a spatula, fold in the coconut until it's just combined. Drop spoonfuls of the batter on the prepared baking sheets, leaving 2 inches between each cookie, as they will spread while cooking.

4. Bake for 12 minutes or until the bottoms are light golden brown. Remove the cookies from the oven and let them cool completely before taking them off the parchment paper.

COOKING TIP **The egg whites will reach a stiff peak better if they are a day old. Make sure they have no shells or egg yolk in them. It's also very important that the bowl is clean and completely dry.**

RICE FLOUR COOKIES

Serves 10
Prep: 20 minutes,
plus overnight to chill
Cook: 15 minutes

1¾ cups powdered sugar

1 pound rice flour

9 ounces vegetable shortening

2 large eggs

1 tablespoon rosewater

1 teaspoon ground cardamom

1 tablespoon poppy seeds

VEGETARIAN Nan Berenji is a popular cookie for Norooz. In Iran, we use a stamp to decorate the tops of the cookies before baking them. You can also just use the tip of a spoon to shape half circles on the cookies. The rice flour gives them a very pleasant aroma that will fill the kitchen while they bake. Rice flour should be fresh and fragrant and completely white in color. It's best to buy it from Asian or Middle Eastern grocery stores.

1. Sift the powdered sugar and rice flour separately into different bowls.

2. Combine the shortening and powdered sugar in a large bowl and beat them together using an electric mixer or a wire whisk until the mixture turns a light cream color.

3. Add the eggs, one at a time, and beat them until they are fully combined. Mix in the rosewater. Add the rice flour to the mixture and mix gently until all the ingredients are well incorporated.

4. Divide the dough in half and shape each half into a disk. Wrap the disks in plastic and refrigerate the dough for at least 12 or up to 24 hours.

5. Preheat the oven to 350°F. Line two baking sheets with parchment paper.

6. Take the dough out of the refrigerator and let it sit for 15 minutes to come to room temperature. Pull off small pieces of dough and use your hands to shape them into balls. Place the cookies on the baking sheets, press them gently with a cookie stamp or the back of a spoon, and sprinkle them with the poppy seeds. Bake for 15 minutes, until the bottoms are very light brown. Remove the cookies from the oven and let them cool on the baking sheets for about 20 minutes, then transfer them to a serving plate.

7. These cookies will stay fresh in an airtight container for up to 10 days.

BEYOND THE BASICS Sifting the rice flour and powdered sugar will definitely boost the quality of the cookies, so don't skip that step. For more fragrant cookies, add 1 teaspoon ground cardamom to the dough in step 3.

PERSIAN CRÊPES WITH SYRUP

خاگینه (قیقاناخ) GHEYGHANAKH

Serves 4
Prep: 5 minutes
Cook: 7 minutes

2 large eggs

2 tablespoons whole milk

2 tablespoons
all-purpose flour

1 tablespoon vegetable oil

½ cup grape molasses

VEGETARIAN, QUICK & EASY This dish is famous in Tabriz, the city in northwestern Iran where my father was born. Gheyghanakh is traditionally served with grape molasses, an ancient sweetener made from reduced grapes. (You can find it in Greek and Middle Eastern grocery stores.) Some people sprinkle chopped walnuts and cinnamon on top before rolling the crêpes.

1. Crack the eggs into a large bowl and beat them with an electric mixer or wire whisk until foamy. Add the milk and flour, and beat until everything is well combined and the batter is smooth.

2. Heat the vegetable oil in a large nonstick skillet over medium heat. Pour all of the batter into the pan and cook for 2 to 3 minutes on each side, until golden brown. Using a spatula, cut the crêpe into eight wedges in the pan and pour the molasses over the top. Reduce the heat to low and cook for 1 minute, until the crêpe has absorbed the molasses. Serve warm.

SUBSTITUTION TIP If you can't get grape molasses, plain molasses would also work well. You can also make a syrup using ¼ cup sugar, ¼ cup water, and 1 tablespoon bloomed saffron. Simmer the sugar and water in a saucepan until it thickens, then add the bloomed saffron. Let the syrup cool completely before pouring it over the crêpe.

PUMPKIN PANCAKES

كاكا KAKA

Serves 6
Prep: 5 minutes,
plus 1 hour for chilling
Cook: 30 minutes

½ cup sugar

1 large egg, at room
temperature

3 tablespoons rosewater

1 cup pumpkin purée

1 cup all-purpose flour

1 teaspoon baking powder

½ teaspoon ground cinnamon

2 tablespoons vegetable oil

1 tablespoon powdered sugar

½ cup chopped walnuts
and pistachios

VEGETARIAN Kaka is a delicious pumpkin pancake from the north of Iran, usually topped with chopped pistachios and walnuts. It's a great dessert, and it also makes for a nutritious breakfast. This pancake is sweet on its own, so there's no need for syrup. It's better to let the batter sit in the refrigerator for 1 hour before making the pancakes, so the flavors blend and the pancakes will hold their shape.

1. Combine the sugar and egg in a large bowl and beat them together using an electric mixer or wire whisk. Add the rosewater and pumpkin purée and beat until smooth. Add the flour, baking powder, and cinnamon, and mix well. Let the batter sit in the refrigerator for 1 hour.

2. Heat the vegetable oil in a large nonstick skillet over medium heat. Pour in ¼ cup of batter for each pancake. Cook each pancake for 2 to 3 minutes per side, until they are browned and springy to the touch.

3. Serve warm topped with powdered sugar, walnuts, and pistachios.

INGREDIENT TIP To make fresh pumpkin purée, bake pumpkin pieces in the oven at 400°F for 1 hour or until very tender, then scoop off the flesh and mash it using a food processor or a potato masher. You can also use canned pumpkin purée instead of fresh—just make sure not to use pumpkin pie filling.

SAFFRON SYRUP CAKE

کیک شربت زعفران KEYK SHARBAT ZAFERAN

Serves 8
Prep: 1 hour
Cook: 20 minutes

FOR THE CAKE

1 cup whole milk

1 tablespoon freshly squeezed lemon juice

4 large eggs, at room temperature

1 cup sugar

½ cup vegetable oil

2 cups all-purpose flour

1½ teaspoons baking powder

1 teaspoon ground cardamom

2 tablespoons ground pistachios

3 tablespoons unsweetened shredded coconut

VEGETARIAN, WORTH THE WAIT Keyk Sharbat Zaferan is a basic cake that is soaked in saffron and rosewater syrup. The cake itself also has a dash of ground cardamom in it, which makes a perfect combination with the syrup. For the full experience, serve it with Persian Brewed Tea (page 190).

TO MAKE THE CAKE

1. Preheat the oven to 350°F. Line a 9-by-13-inch baking dish with parchment paper.

2. Mix the milk and lemon juice in a small bowl. Set it aside for 5 minutes.

3. In a large bowl, using an electric mixer or a wire whisk, beat the eggs until foamy. Beat or whisk in the sugar until it is fully combined, then add the oil and the lemon juice–milk mixture. Beat for 1 minute.

4. Add the flour, baking powder, and ground cardamom. Stir gently using a spatula until just combined.

5. Pour the batter into the prepared baking dish and bake for 20 minutes or until a tester toothpick comes out clean.

6. Remove the cake from the oven and let it cool to room temperature.

7. When the cake is cool, use a sharp knife to cut it into 1½-inch-wide strips, then cut on the diagonal so you have diamond-shaped cake pieces. Don't take the pieces out of the pan.

FOR THE SYRUP

1 cup sugar

1 cup water

4 tablespoons bloomed saffron (see page 21)

2 tablespoons rosewater

8. Gently spoon the cooled syrup slowly over the cake. The cake will absorb the syrup right away. Use enough syrup so every part of the cake is soaked, but don't use so much that it is sodden.

9. Top the cake with the ground pistachios and shredded coconut. Gently take the cake pieces out of the baking pan and place them on individual plates.

10. Serve with Persian Brewed Tea (page 190).

TO MAKE THE SYRUP

1. While the cake bakes, combine the sugar and water in a small saucepan over medium heat. Bring the mixture to a simmer, stirring frequently, then stir in the bloomed saffron and rosewater. Simmer for 2 minutes, then remove the pan from the heat.

2. Let the syrup cool to room temperature. Make sure both the cake and the syrup are at room temperature before cutting the cake. If either one is warm, the cake will fall apart and get mushy.

INGREDIENT TIP Good-quality ground pistachios have a nice green color and are not dark. You can make your own ground pistachios by grinding them in a coffee grinder. Make sure the coffee grinder is completely clean before grinding the nuts.

Acknowledgments

This book became what it is with the help of many people around me. I would like to thank my editor, Clara Song Lee, for being so helpful and compassionate, and for giving me a chance to show my love and passion for food and writing. While most Persian cookbooks consist of only the most popular Persian foods, Clara led me to write about homey Persian food, true food that is made in a true family in the simplest way possible. I would like to thank the team at Rockridge Press for being so creative and passionate about what they do and the great work they put into making this book come to life.

While writing this book, I talked to my friends and family to make sure each recipe is authentic, and I would like to thank them for their thoughts. Writing this book made me love Persian food more than I ever had in my entire life.

I would like to thank my husband and my best friend, Kyle, without whom I would not have had the courage and power to start the food blog that led me to write this book. Thank you, Kyle, for always being there with me when I needed a powerful voice to tell me that I can do this. I'm thankful to all my family in Iran, who were always there for me even with an almost 12-hour time difference. I'm grateful to my family and my in-laws for believing in me and supporting me in pursuing my dream and offering me help at every stage of my career.

And a large thank you to my maman, for making the best Persian food in the world and having me fall in love with cooking and baking every day over and over again. Thank you, maman jan, for making food for us every single day with love and passion. Thank you for being my partner when we made 200 pounds of cookies in a week for our Norooz sale, and thank you for always telling me that dreams do come true.

Menus for Holidays & Celebrations

AROOSI—A PERSIAN WEDDING

The same as everywhere else, weddings are a big deal in Iran. You want everything to be perfect and the food to be fantastic. You want to make sure the caterer is doing a great job, because people know good food in Iran and you don't want poor-quality food at your wedding. Weddings in Iran are large and have many different types of food, from kabobs to polos, to desserts, and of course the cake. What does a typical wedding menu look like?

Yogurt & Cucumber
Mast-o-Khiar, p. 30

Yogurt & Eggplant
Borani Bademjaan, p. 31

Oatmeal Soup
Soope Jo, p. 68

Chicken with Tomato Sauce
Khorak-e-Morgh, p. 98

Saffron Chicken
Morgh-e-Zaferani, p. 100

Lamb Shanks
Khorak-e-Mahicheh, p. 102

Steamed White Rice
Chelo, p. 104

Dill & Fava Bean Rice
Shevid Baghali Polo, p. 108

Barberry & Saffron Rice
Zereshk Polo, p. 110

Chicken Kabobs
Joojeh Kabob, p. 116

Lamb Kabobs
Kabob Chenjeh, p. 120

Savory Saffron Rice Cake
Tahchin, p. 149

Jeweled Sweet Rice
Morasa Polo, p. 178

NOROOZ—PERSIAN NEW YEAR

Norooz is the first day of spring, which Persians and other people in the region celebrate in March as the start of a new year. For many, this is the most important day of the year, and Iranians usually try to be home with their families for this festival. The night before the new year is a great time to gather and have a special meal. What can be served that night?

Stuffed Fish
Mahi Shekam Por, p. 144

Herbs & Rice
Sabzi Polo, p. 106

Persian Brewed Tea
Chai Dam Kardeh, p. 190

Dried fruits and nuts

Roasted Chickpea Flour Cookies
Shirini Nokhodchi, p. 205

Rice Flour Cookies
Nan Berenji, p. 208

Coconut Sweets
Loz-e Nargil, p. 198

Persian Rosettes
Nan Panjereh-i, p. 203

SHAB-E YALDA—THE LONGEST NIGHT OF THE YEAR

This beautiful celebration is spent with family and loved ones at home, celebrating the fact that the longest night is passing and after it, the days are going to be longer. For this December night, families gather, have dinner, and stay awake late—reading poems, eating nuts, and definitely eating pomegranate and watermelon to say good-bye to the warmer weather and welcome winter into their homes. What would be a good menu for Shab-e Yalda?

Stuffed Fish
Mahi Shekam Por, p. 144

Herbs & Rice
Sabzi Polo, p. 106

Cucumber & Tomato Salad
Salad Shirazi, p. 40

Pomegranate & Walnut Meatballs
Koofteh Anar-o-Gerdoo, p. 134

Saffron & Rose Tea
Chai Zafran va Gol, p. 189

Dried fruits and nuts

Pomegranate seeds and Watermelon

Measurement Conversions

VOLUME EQUIVALENTS (LIQUID)

US STANDARD	US STANDARD (OUNCES)	METRIC (APPROXIMATE)
2 tablespoons	1 fl. oz.	30 mL
¼ cup	2 fl. oz.	60 mL
½ cup	4 fl. oz.	120 mL
1 cup	8 fl. oz.	240 mL
1½ cups	12 fl. oz.	355 mL
2 cups or 1 pint	16 fl. oz.	475 mL
4 cups or 1 quart	32 fl. oz.	1 L
1 gallon	128 fl. oz.	4 L

OVEN TEMPERATURES

FAHRENHEIT	CELSIUS (APPROXIMATE)
250°F	120°C
300°F	150°C
325°F	165°C
350°F	180°C
375°F	190°C
400°F	200°C
425°F	220°C
450°F	230°C

VOLUME EQUIVALENTS (DRY)

US STANDARD	METRIC (APPROXIMATE)
⅛ teaspoon	0.5 mL
¼ teaspoon	1 mL
½ teaspoon	2 mL
¾ teaspoon	4 mL
1 teaspoon	5 mL
1 tablespoon	15 mL
¼ cup	59 mL
⅓ cup	79 mL
½ cup	118 mL
⅔ cup	156 mL
¾ cup	177 mL
1 cup	235 mL
2 cups or 1 pint	475 mL
3 cups	700 mL
4 cups or 1 quart	1 L

WEIGHT EQUIVALENTS

US STANDARD	METRIC (APPROXIMATE)
½ ounce	15 g
1 ounce	30 g
2 ounces	60 g
4 ounces	115 g
8 ounces	225 g
12 ounces	340 g
16 ounces or 1 pound	455 g

Resources

GROCERY STORES

To find grocery stores in your area, search Google.com or Yelp.com for "Persian supermarket," "Mediterranean supermarket," and "Middle Eastern supermarket."

ONLINE RETAILERS

Amazon
www.amazon.com

Indian Foods Company
www.indianfoodsco.com
(look in the Ethnic Grocery Store section)

Kalamala
www.kalamala.com

Kalyustan's
kalustyans.com

Persian Basket
persianbasket.com

Sadaf Foods
www.sadaf.com

Recipe Index

Index

About the Author

SHADI HASANZADENEMATI is the recipe developer, author, and photographer behind the blog *Unicorns in the Kitchen*. For Shadi, the magic of cooking is in bringing everyone together and sharing the experience. She believes that a recipe is like a canvas and the person who makes it is the artist, bringing their own creativity to give it a personal twist. At *Unicorns in the Kitchen*, Shadi writes about all varieties of food, from cookies and comfort dishes to traditional Persian favorites. Learn more at UnicornsInTheKitchen.com.

CPSIA information can be obtained
at www.ICGtesting.com
Printed in the USA
LVHW071600141222
735233LV00007B/186

9 781623 157630